DUNS SCOTUS LIBRARY
LOURDES COLLEGE
SYLVANIA, OHIO

3 0379 1002

D0078203

WITHDRAWN

WOMEN DRUG USERS

WOMEN DRUG USERS

*An Ethnography of a
Female Injecting Community*

AVRIL TAYLOR

CLARENDON PRESS · OXFORD

94-789

Oxford University Press, Walton Street, Oxford OX2 6DP

Oxford New York Toronto
Delhi Bombay Calcutta Madras Karachi
Kuala Lumpur Singapore Hong Kong Tokyo
Nairobi Dar es Salaam Cape Town
Melbourne Auckland Madrid
and associated companies in
Berlin Ibadan

Oxford is a trade mark of Oxford University Press

Published in the United States
by Oxford University Press Inc., New York

© Avril Taylor 1993

First published 1993

All rights reserved. No part of this publication may be reproduced,
stored in a retrieval system, or transmitted, in any form or by any means,
without the prior permission in writing of Oxford University Press.
Within the UK, exceptions are allowed in respect of any fair dealing for the
purpose of research or private study, or criticism or review, as permitted
under the Copyright, Designs and Patents Act, 1988, or in the case of
reprographic reproduction in accordance with the terms of the licences
issued by the Copyright Licensing Agency. Enquiries concerning
reproduction outside these terms and in other countries should be
sent to the Rights Department, Oxford University Press,
at the address above.

This book is sold subject to the condition that it shall not, by way
of trade or otherwise, be lent, re-sold, hired out or otherwise circulated
without the publisher's prior consent in any form of binding or cover
other than that in which it is published and without a similar condition
including this condition being imposed on the subsequent purchaser

British Library Cataloguing in Publication Data
Data available

Library of Congress Cataloging in Publication Data
Data available
ISBN 0-19-825796-1

3 5 7 9 10 8 6 4 2

Printed and bound in Great Britain by
Biddles Ltd, Guildford and King's Lynn

For my mother

Acknowledgements

Several people helped me in various ways to complete the Ph.D. thesis upon which this book is based. First and foremost my thanks go to the women who shared their experiences with me and allowed me into their lives for fifteen months. Without them, this book could not have been written. The male drug users I encountered also deserve mention for their friendly acceptance of my presence within their community. I would also like to thank David Carmichael, whose assistance and support were appreciated throughout and beyond the period of fieldwork. Grace and John Smith, Pat Gilligan and Jimmy Mitchell all contributed to making the period of fieldwork an enjoyable experience.

The University of Glasgow funded my research, for which I am grateful. Ruth Madigan was an invaluable supervisor, consistently giving encouragement, constructive criticism, and advice. I am also extremely grateful to Jason Ditton for his constant encouragement in my research efforts. He, too, provided meticulous supervision, and was always ready to provide both practical and intellectual assistance.

My thanks also go to Kathleen Davidson, Pip Townsend, Barbara Perry, and Mary Snaddon, who all typed faultless transcriptions of interviews which were taped in less than ideal conditions.

Last, but certainly not least, I wish to thank my family. My husband, Ian, and my sons, Michael, Kevin, David, and Derek, not only uncomplainingly put up with the considerable disruption to their lives caused by the research for this book, but also provided real and much appreciated help. Between them, they read and reread endless drafts, gave helpful comments, compiled the bibliography, and proof-read the final manuscript. Most of all, they continually provided moral support and inspired me with confidence to complete the final product.

Contents

1

Introduction

This book provides an account of the lives and experiences of a group of female intravenous drug users in Glasgow. It is based on fifteen months' participant observation of the women in their own setting and on in-depth interviews carried out at the end of the observation period. It is the first full ethnographic account of the lifestyle of female drug users.[1]

Very little sociological research has been directed at female illicit drug users. Most research in the field of illicit drug use has over-whelmingly concentrated on young male users, and females are either ignored or seen as marginal (Blenheim Project, 1988; File, 1976; Gomberg, 1986; Jeffries, 1983; Marsh 1982; Prather and Fidell, 1978; Women 2000, 1987). Explanations for this lack of attention to women drug users typically come in two forms: that there are very few women illicit drug users (Auld, 1986; Ellinwood, 1966; Martin and Martin, 1980; McGrath, 1982; Polit, 1976); and that women's experience of drug use is the same as men's (Christmas, 1978; Ettore, 1985; 1986; 1989a; Fuller, 1978; Gomberg, 1986; Martin and Martin, 1980; News Release, 1979; Ray and Braude, 1986; Women 2000, 1987). Such explanations, implying that women are not worth studying as a separate group, are no longer applicable, however—if, indeed, they ever were.

The argument that women drug users are few in number, and that therefore illicit drug use is essentially an activity indulged in by males, can be and has been challenged. Official statistics on Scottish drug users show that numbers of new female users are increasing each year (Ditton and Taylor, 1987). A survey of drug agencies in Scotland revealed a male to female ratio of new drug using clients of 1.5 : 1 (Ditton and Taylor, 1990). Others have pointed out the increase in numbers of women who use illicit substances (Doshan and Bursch, 1982; Kaestner *et al.*, 1986; Polit *et*

---

[1] The terms 'drug use(rs)' in this work refers solely to *illicit* drug use.

al., 1976; Reed, 1985; Smithberg and Westermeyer, 1985; Tyler and Thompson, 1980). The second argument, that women's experience of drug use is similar to that of men's, can also be questioned on the basis of feminist research, which has shown that women and men typically experience social situations differently (Ettore, 1986; Reed, 1985).

Findings such as these have led to repeated calls for studies focusing on the particular experiences of women drug users (see e.g. Christmas, 1978; Cohen *et al.*, 1989; Cuskey, 1982; Dorn and South, 1987; Ellinwood *et al.*, 1966; Ettore, 1986; 1989*a*; 1989*b*; Feldman, 1968; Fuller, 1978; Gerstein *et al.*, 1979; Hanson *et al.*, 1985; Parker *et al.*, 1988; Polit *et al.*, 1976; Prather, 1981; Tyler and Thompson, 1980; Women 2000, 1987). Yet to date only one sociological study has examined in depth how drug use fits into the lives of women (Rosenbaum, 1981). Despite this notable study, what this means in practice is that little has changed to alter the views put forward in 1979 that 'the extent, context and experience of female drug use remain invisible' (Perry, 1979: 4), and that the particular problems faced by women are ignored (News Release, 1979).

Images of the Female Illicit Drug-User

Women drug users, however, have not been totally neglected in the literature. There is a vast amount written on the use of drugs by women, but much of it is medical, psychiatric, or psychological in orientation (Rosenbaum, 1981). In particular, the effect of drug use on women's reproduction has been focused upon, with the emphasis frequently on the foetus and newborn infant (see Chapter 5). In addition, women have been directly compared with men or considered as a subset of the larger male population (Chein *et al.*, 1964; De Leon, 1974; Ellinwood *et al.*, 1966; Gossop, 1986; Griffin-Shelley, 1986; Hser *et al.*, 1987; Ross *et al.*, 1988; Waldorf, 1973). The relationship between drug use and female criminality has been examined (see Chapter 3), as well as issues pertinent to the treatment of female drug users (Cuskey, 1982; Dorn and South, 1985; Doshan and Bursch, 1982; Eldred and Washington, 1976; Johnson Institute, 1989; Levy and Doyle, 1975; MacGregor and Ettore, 1987; Marsh, 1982; Mandel *et al.*, 1979; Mondanaro, 1989; Reed, 1985; Ryan and Moise, 1979; Schultz, 1974; Tyler and Thompson, 1980).

The predominant view of women drug users which emanates from much research is that they are 'pathetic, passive, psychologically or socially inadequate' (Perry, 1979: 1). In comparison with male drug users, they have been portrayed as having less will-power and being morally weaker (Densen-Gerber *et al.*, 1972; Mondanaro, 1989: 10), 'sicker' (Gomberg, 1986; Kaufman, 1985; Levy and Doyle, 1975; Marsh *et al.*, 1982; Marsh and Simpson, 1986; Mondanaro, 1989; News Release, 1979; Polit *et al.*, 1976; Reed, 1985) more deviant (Christmas, 1978; Ettore, 1987; Gomberg, 1986; Peak and Glankoff, 1975; Perry, 1979; Women 2000, 1987), and more emotional and psychologically disordered (see Chein *et al.*, 1964; Christmas, 1978; Cuskey, 1982; Densen-Gerber *et al.*, 1972; De Leon, 1974; d'Orban, 1970; Gossop, 1986; Levy and Doyle, 1975; Marsh *et al.*, 1982; Perry, 1979; Polit *et al.*, 1976; Women 2000, 1987). They have been regarded as excessively dependent (see Auld *et al.*, 1986; Carr, 1975; Cuskey, 1982; Howard and Borges, 1970; Kaufman, 1985; Levy and Doyle, 1975; NIDA, 1979; News Release, 1979; Silver *et al.*, 1975; Sutter, 1966; Tucker, 1979; Wellisch *et al.*, 1970), as exemplified in the notion that women users are introduced to drug use by male partners (see Chapter 2) and rely on them for their drug supplies. This latter view has been challenged, however, by some who argue that women are becoming more assertive and independent in maintaining their drug habit (see Chapter 3). Despite their deviant way of life, it has been argued that women drug users themselves hold traditional values (Baldinger *et al.*, 1972; Colten, 1979; Cuskey, 1982; Parker *et al.*, 1988; Polit *et al.*, 1976; Rosenbaum, 1981; Suffet and Brotman, 1976), and the conflict between their attitudes and their deviant lifestyle leads them to experience low self-esteem (Cuskey, 1982; Colten, 1979; Dorn and South, 1985; Finnegan, 1981; Gossop, 1986; Griffin-Shelley, 1986; NIDA, 1979; Reed, 1985; Silver *et al.*, 1975; Stewart, 1987). The career of women drug users has been seen in terms of 'narrowing options' (Rosenbaum, 1981) in which the practice of traditional ways of living become increasingly closed off to them. They have been viewed as lonely and isolated (Cuskey, 1982; Kroll, 1986; NIDA, 1979; Ottenberg, 1975), sexually deviant (Densen-Gerber *et al.*, 1972), 'polluted' (Ettore, 1987; 1989*a*; 1989*b*; Wolfson and Murray, 1986), and inadequate, unfit mothers (see Chapter 5).

Most of these conclusions have been based on interviews with women in treatment. It has been argued, however, that the form of questions in many such interviews reveals stereotypical assumptions of acceptable feminine behaviour (Schultz, 1974). Assumptions found within questionnaires can also 'produce a falsely concrete body of data which distorts rather than reflects actors' meanings' (Maynard, 1990: 274). Moreover, the respondents' representative-ness of female drug users in general is also open to question, as women drug users are proportionately less likely than their male counterparts to come to the attention of treatment centres (Advisory Council on the Misuse of Drugs, 1989; Henderson, 1990; Parker *et al.*, 1988). Where studies have investigated the social setting of women drug users, they have usually concentrated on one aspect of an illicit drug using lifestyle (see e.g. File, 1976), and as a result are similar to treatment-based interviews in that they ignore the social setting and social relationships within which drug use takes place.

Currently, most of the literature comes from the United States and much of it is dated. Since the beginning of the 1980s and the discovery of the new 'heroin epidemic' (Ditton and Speirits, 1984; Drummond, 1986) amongst young working-class people in Britain, sociologists have begun to turn their attention to this phenomenon (see e.g. Dorn and South, 1987; McKeganey and Boddy, 1987; Morrison, 1989; O'Bryan, 1989; Parker *et al.*, 1988; Pearson, 1987*a*; 1987*b*; Pearson *et al.*, 1986; Stewart, 1987). These more recent studies acknowledge to a somewhat greater extent the existence of women, even if only by recognizing sex as a variable. Some point out the need to explain drug use by women but do not themselves take up the challenge (Dorn and South, 1985; 1987; Ettore, 1986; 1987; 1989*a*; 1989*b*; Parker *et al.*, 1988).

The discovery of the prevalence amongst intravenous drug users of the HIV virus which leads to AIDS has also brought women drug users into focus; but here again, with a few notable excep-tions (Henderson, 1990; Richardson, 1987; Women and AIDS, 1988; Women, HIV/AIDS Network, 1989), the attention has been con-centrated on the effect on reproduction (see e.g. Scottish Drugs Forum, 1989), thus re-emphasizing the medical viewpoint on women. Indeed, one recent Scottish study refers only to the increas-ing number of women drug users in terms of the potential likeli-hood of increasing numbers of their children being born infected with the AIDS virus (Robertson, 1987).

A little change is perceptible, however. Studies are beginning to appear written by women and aimed at women drug users them-selves, as well as a wider audience. These writings with a mainly feminist focus discuss practical implications of drug use, such as those related to women's health (Blenheim Project, 1988; Ettore, 1986; 1987; 1989*a*; 1989*b*; O'Donohue and Richardson, 1984; Wolfson and Murray, 1986). In addition, however, they attempt to relate drug use to women's role and status in society, a development for which there have been repeated calls (Auld *et al.*, 1986; Dorn and South, 1985; Ettore, 1987; 1989*a*; 1989*b*; Fuller, 1978; Marsh *et al.*, 1982; Parker *et al.*, 1988; Suffet and Brotman, 1976; Women 2000, 1987). Whilst these are welcome signs, they still represent only a tiny minority of the studies of women's drug use and do not discuss the subject in any great depth. Most studies still 'relate only to pregnancy, childbirth and the ability to care for children' (Blenheim Project, 1988: 1). The stereotype of women drug users still remains as that of 'polluted' (Ettore, 1989*a*; 1989*b*), immature (Bury, 1988) women who are 'necessarily chaotic, out of control of their own lives and unfit to be in charge of anyone else's' (Perry, 1987: 6). In short, they are portrayed as 'untrustworthy, immature, promiscuous, irresponsible, inadequate, unnatural, unfit mothers' whose drug use is regarded as 'symptomatic of an inadequate personality' (Wolfson and Murray, 1986: 8).

What Is Missing

From the United States there has arisen a notable tradition of ethnographic studies which have produced valuable insights into the lives of illicit drug users (Agar, 1973; Feldman, 1968; Fiddle, 1976; Finestone, 1957; Hanson *et al.*, 1985; Hughes *et al.*, 1971; Johnson *et al.*, 1985; Preble and Casey, 1969; Sutter, 1966; Waldorf, 1973; Williams, 1989). Based on the application of the notion of 'career',[2] which allows drug use to be viewed non-judgementally as a process, these studies have provided in-depth knowledge of what it is like to be a drug user from the perspective of drug users themselves. What characterizes such studies is that they take into account the social and cultural context in which drug use occurs and, viewing drug use from the point of view of the drug user, show the meaning that drug use has in their lives. But, with the exception of Rosenbaum's study (1981), all look at the career of the male drug user, and have little or nothing to say about female drug users.

From such studies of drug users in their social setting, the male

---

[2] For further discussion see Becker (1963) and Rubington (1967).

drug user has come to be characterized as a purposeful, resourceful person responding in a rational manner to particular sets of social circumstances. These circumstances were shaped by the lack of legitimate career opportunities available to those young men in the slum areas which most of them inhabited. The lifestyle associated with drug use allowed these young men to develop an alternative career which provided them with meaning, motivation, and status. What was important about such an approach was that the findings were in direct opposition to previous traditional treatment-based research which had characterized male drug use an escapist activity, one in which users were regarded as pathetic and weak (Chein *et al.*, 1964; Cloward and Ohlin, 1960).

In Britain in the 1980s, the concept of 'career' has been adopted and adapted in attempts to understand the use of heroin and other illicit drugs by young people in working-class areas (Auld *et al.*, 1986; Cousins and Bentall, 1989; Gilman, 1988; Parker *et al.*, 1988; Pearson, 1987*a*; 1987*b*; 1988; Pearson *et al.*, 1986). In the wake of high unemployment and lack of legitimate job opportunities, it is argued that the lifestyle associated with illicit drug use can provide meaning and purpose in an otherwise meaningless and purposeless existence (Auld *et al.*, 1986; Gilman, 1988; Pearson, 1987*a*; 1987*b*; 1988; Pearson *et al.*, 1986; Peck and Plant, 1986; Unell, 1987). In this regard, the lifestyle of the male drug user has been compared to that of the professional soldier (Gilman, 1988). Whilst women are given a higher profile in these more recent British studies, their experiences are either implicitly regarded as the same as men's or, at best, are afforded a few paragraphs in which their special problems, particularly related to pregnancy and childbirth, are considered.

One can speculate on the reasons for the marginalization of women in such studies,[3] but the result of this lack of attention is that, like Hanson *et al.*'s inner-city black male drug users, 'little systematic knowledge has emerged regarding the relationship between the social contexts within which they live, their own view of their social worlds and their drug use' (1985: 6). No full ethnographic study of female drug users has been undertaken anywhere until now. The single major study of women drug users to date was conducted using only in-depth interviews with paid informants

---

[3] e.g. Polit *et al.* (1976: 9) quote Eldred Washington (1975) as commenting that the amount of research in any given area is a fairly good 'unobtrusive measure' of the degree of interest which that topic holds for a scientific community.

(Rosenbaum, 1981). Data collected in this fashion are methodologically flawed, however, in that, as Polsky argues, they are 'data that are too heavily retrospective; data from people that are not really free to put you down ... data from someone who is not behaving as [she] normally would in [her] normal life-situations; and, above all, data that you cannot supplement with, or interpret in the light of your own direct observation of the criminal's natural behaviour in [her] natural environment' (Polsky, 1969: 121).

What This Study Does

A contemporary empirical account is presented here of the lives and experiences of a group of intravenous female drug users in Glasgow. The goal was a more complete and informed image of female drug users than those produced hitherto. Much of the text allows the women to speak for themselves, describing from their point of view the lifestyles which have evolved around their use of illicit drugs. From their accounts we discover how and why they became involved in using illicit substances; how they typically spend each day; how they finance their drug use; with whom they socialize; how they care for their children; their satisfaction or otherwise with their lifestyle; their prospects for relinquishing their drug careers if they so wish; to whom they turn for help; and their perceptions of treatment options.

The research was planned and carried out within the tradition of urban ethnography. The basic theoretical orientation is provided by Weber's theory of 'social action' and his *verstehen* sociology of interpretative understanding (Weber, 1947). Basically this means that in order to understand social actions we must grasp the meanings that actors attach to their actions. The methodological approach has also been informed by the symbolic interactionist perspective, central to which is (again) the concept of 'meaning' and particularly the variability of meaning in everyday life (Blumer, 1969; Mead, 1939). It has been said that 'the real strength of the symbolic interactionism approach lies not so much in its theoretical foundations as in the practical qualitative research that the approach has generated ... qualitative research methods that aim "to get in where the action is" and "tell it like it is" from the perspective of those involved' (Bilton *et al.*, 1981).

We have seen how such methods have been used in studies of

male drug users and have been instrumental in producing a view of drug using lifestyles from the drug users' own perspective, in particular showing the meaning that drug use has for them. In the process this approach helped change the view of male drug use as individual pathological behaviour to a view in which the social situation of drug users and overall social structure were seen as significant.

Similarly, as I hope to demonstrate, by applying this approach to female drug users, new insights and alternative understandings begin to emerge. Against the stereotypical view of pathetic, inadequate individuals, women drug users in this study are shown to be rational, active people making decisions based on the contingencies of both their drug using careers and their roles and status in society. Such an approach also allows the ordinariness as well as the more deviant aspects of their lives to be seen, showing that women drug users have many of the same concerns, fears, and hopes as other women.

The concept of 'career' guides the overall theoretical framework. In addition, the framework is also feminist in perspective, given that feminism assumes 'a perspective in which women's experiences, ideas and needs are valid in their own right' (Duelli Klein, 1983: 89), and is 'an attempt to insist upon the experience and very existence of women' (Roberts, 1981: 15). To this end, much of the text is devoted to allowing the women to speak for themselves, describing their lifestyles in their own words.

Parker *et al.* (1988) have noted the dearth of a British theoretical framework within which to make sense of the new wave of illicit drug use and argue that such a framework will only emerge from substantive studies. Whilst the primary goal of this study is to provide an ethnographic account and analysis of female illicit drug users, I hope, as Preble and Casey did earlier, 'that this contemporary account of the social setting for [illicit drug use] will provide useful data for the modifications of theory and practice' (1969: 3).

Methodological Procedure

The findings of this study are based on fifteen months participant observation of over fifty women and on in-depth interviews with twenty-six women carried out at the end of this period. Eight of these women formed a core group of 'key informants'.

The benefits of participant observation as a method for studying deviant groups is well documented. Becker has stated that, for theorizing purposes, 'there are not enough studies to provide us with facts about the lives of deviants as they live them. . . . Above all we do not have enough studies in which the person doing the research has achieved close contact with those [the researcher] studies' (Becker, 1963: 163–8). He added, 'To get an accurate and complete account of what addicts do, what their patterns of association are and so on, [the researcher] must spend at least some time observing them in their "natural habitat" as they go about their ordinary activities' (p. 170). Douglas has also argued that it is 'only by getting inside deviant groups and by experiencing things the way they do [that] we can ever come to see how deviants really view the world' (1972: 4).

As ethnography is 'an approach which avoids the pre-definition of what is to be considered relevant and aims at discovering the insider's view of [her] social world' (Spradley, 1980: 24), it is also particularly suitable for feminist research. Such research has as its aim the uncovering of women's own perspectives of their lives as resources for analysis (S. Harding, 1987: 7); and to achieve this the employment of the 'underclass' approach 'insisting on the importance of "studying up" rather than "studying down", is useful, an approach long used in ethnographic research on male deviant groups' (see e.g. Becker, 1970*a*).

As discussed above, several researchers have undertaken ethnographic studies and provided us with accounts of the lives of male illicit drug users. However, no ethnographic study of female drug users alone has been undertaken anywhere. As an initial step towards overcoming this failure to study women drug users in their natural environment, for fifteen months I spent most of my days, and many nights, participating in and observing the activities of a group of female injecting drug users in an area of Glasgow.

Douglas has argued that 'essays on methods, such as the classical one by William Foote Whyte concerning his methods of observation that led to *Street Corner Society*, must become far more detailed and far more integral to the reporting of the study. Only in these ways will we be able to adequately judge the validity of the observations and to attempt to reproduce studies to see if similar methods of studying similar groups produce similar findings' (Douglas, 1972: 32–3; Whyte, 1945). Yet Mann argues that 'the experiences of field workers have not been systematically reported and as a result a whole area of methodological skills has remained relatively uncodified' (1970: 119). These charges remain accurate, particularly in the field of researching illicit drug use by means of participant observation. Very few researchers provide clear details of how they carried this out. The remainder of this chapter is an attempt to fill this gap by describing in some detail how the data for this thesis were collected, and by highlighting the practical issues and problems encountered in the use of this particular method.

Gaining Access

Having decided on the topic of study and the method to be used, the researcher is faced with deciding, first, where to carry out the research and, second, how to gain access to the chosen site.

My previous knowledge of the intravenous drug scene in Glasgow had indicated four areas which would be useful for my purposes. However, just as Whyte chose Cornerville, for his study of *Street Corner Society*, for very unscientific reasons (Whyte, 1945: 283), so I *rejected* two of these sites for a similar unscientific reason: I would not have felt safe working on my own in either of these locations. Like Power, I believe that 'personal safety is paramount and no researcher should enter an arena if they feel they may be putting themselves in danger' (Power 1989: 44). The third area was snatched from my grasp by another researcher just as I had begun to negotiate access. This left me having to gain access to number four.

Several issues had to be confronted at this point. Most crucially, how was I to begin to penetrate an area with which I was totally unfamiliar and where I was totally unknown? Should I attempt to do it on my own or should I seek someone who could facilitate my entry? Should the research be carried out overtly or covertly?

At this point I began to panic. I had never, to my knowledge, met, never mind spoken to, an intravenous drug user, and I realized to my shame and horror that, despite all my background reading and my theoretical leanings towards labelling theory, stereotypical images of drug users as portrayed in the media had not been totally eradicated from my mind: I actually felt quite scared about encountering them. I was afraid, too, that, even if my fears proved unfounded, I would be unable to achieve any rapport. To overcome this hurdle, I accompanied a colleague on his research visits to a drug agency in another part of the city, where I met several drug users: my fears were indeed unfounded.

This brought me back to the problem of how to gain access to my chosen area.

The ethics and practical issues surrounding covert versus overt research are discussed in most texts on research methods, and better than here. There is one glaringly obvious reason why researchers in the drug field must do open research: unless one is or has been an intravenous drug user, it would be extremely difficult to pass as one. Although I had already familiarized myself, through background reading and through discussion with researchers who had been involved in survey research in the city, with the methods of buying and selling and using drugs intravenously, and whilst agreeing with Malinowski that 'it is good for the ethnographer sometimes ... to join in what is going on', as this allows the researcher to obtain an understanding of the lives of those being studied (Malinowski, 1922: 21), there were certain limits beyond which I was not prepared to go. I was also mindful of Polsky's advice to those engaged in the study of criminal behaviour that in doing field research on criminals 'you damned well better not pretend to be "one of them" because they will test this claim out and one of two things will happen: either you will ... get sucked into "participant" observation of the sort you would rather not undertake or you will be exposed with still greater negative consequences' (Polsky, 1969: 122).

The decision to be open in my approach (although really I had no choice) led me to seek someone who would introduce me to some drug users in my chosen area. I already knew where the drug users 'hung out', where they did their buying and selling, but I felt that to hang about there as an unknown would invite suspicion not only from my future subjects but also from the police. Moreover, my knowledge extended mainly to the activities of male users. I was not sure if it would be seemly female behaviour to hang about street corners. Also, the hanging about was not always simply hanging about—it was also the way they carried out their business transactions—*not* the occasion upon which to approach and engage them in conversation.

I decided to approach the local detached drug worker. I had been given his name by a mutual acquaintance; but, even knowing that I could use this person's name as an introduction, it was at this stage that I first felt what Hughes has described as a 'torture' (Hughes, 1960: p. iii). As Gans states, 'asking for entry requires the researcher to sell himself to the people whose groups he wishes to enter', (Gans, 1982: 57) which is something I disliked doing.

Choosing a sponsor presents certain difficulties in any research operation, unless you know the person well beforehand, which was not the case in this study. I did not know if the drug worker was regarded in a favourable light by the women drug users in the area. I wondered, therefore, if he would limit me in any way. Would he expect information from me about the women in exchange for his introductions? I knew that I had to make clear at the outset that, whilst I would be grateful for the introductions, I could not offer in exchange any information about the women. Another consideration was what to tell him of the research: at this stage my research aims were still vague. But I was lucky in my choice of sponsor. He had a particular interest in women users, felt that not enough attention was paid to them and their problems, and was glad to welcome a researcher who would highlight this. He was accepted and trusted by the women, and he was willing and able to accept that I would not pass any data on to him. What *he* wanted was to have a woman around to whom he could refer his clients if they felt the need to talk to a female. He agreed to introduce me to some users, and to accompany me around the area for at least my first few visits.

In the Field

The area in which I carried out the research was typical of many inner-city areas: poverty, unemployment, and poor-quality housing were pervasive. In an area always associated with slum housing, the old tenements have been replaced with post-war, high-rise concrete flats, some of which had to be demolished, because of poor construction, when less than twenty years old, leaving a gaping wasteland on the edge of the community. The first impression is one of dirty, dusty streets overshadowed by grey concrete, intermittently relieved by a school, a church, a few groups of terraced houses, and the occasional tree.

My first days in this area are remembered as a confusing kaleido-scope of sights, sounds, and feelings. The feelings can be summed up in one word—anxiety. This anxiety was engendered by three methodological concerns: the impression I was making; how I would collect my data; and what data to collect.

My first excursion was to a drug drop-in centre catering for both drug users and alcoholics, a place where drug users could drop in for a chat with staff, meet other users, have a coffee, and seek help and advice when needed. I had earlier decided that, unless I felt that it was appropriate and not obstructive, I would not take notes in the presence of anyone. This decision arose partly from my fear that note-taking would invite suspicion and would hinder my acceptance, and partly from the role I was hoping to adopt.

Gold has written of four types of participant observer. My method resembles most closely his 'participant-as-observer' role—one where the observer 'develops relationships with informants through time and where [she] is apt to spend more time and energy par-ticipating than observing' (1969: 35). In other words, I wanted to be accepted as an acquaintance, if not a friend—a relationship not likely to be fostered by continuous note-taking. My plan was, there-fore, to write up field notes at the end of each day (which was the method used throughout fieldwork) and to supplement my parti-cipant observer data by in-depth interviews towards the end of fieldwork. At first I was anxious that I would not remember any-thing, but was quickly surprised at how good my recall proved to be.

I had given much thought to my own 'impression management' before attempting to gain access. The dressing styles of the drug users I had met in the clinic setting—jeans, sweatshirts, T-shirts —did not differ much from university dress—so that did not pre-sent much of a problem. I knew that I would be older than most of my informants, but there was nothing I could do about that. As my contacts ranged in age from teenagers to women in their thirties, I believe that my age had no detrimental effect on data collection, and indeed have come to agree with Wax that 'the most advant-ageous and rewarding situation [for a researcher] is probably that of a mature woman', if only because the wider experience of older women enables empathy across a greater range of experiences (1979: 514).

I had also been told by a social worker that I looked 'too healthy' to be accepted as a drug user. I did not want to *pass* as a drug user, however, but only to be accepted among them, so I did not consider that this would be a drawback. In any event, either my health deteriorated during the research, or the social worker's opinion was invalid: I was mistaken for a 'junkie' on several occasions.

Language, or accent, was another consideration. All my informants were working-class and spoke with broad Glaswegian accents. Being a native Glaswegian, I was aware of the antipathy sometimes caused by a 'posh' accent. I therefore decided that at least a slight modification of my own accent might be wise. However, apart from a few stylistic changes, such as leaving endings off words, and sometimes substituting their words for mine ('wean' instead of 'child', for example), I stuck to my own speech style. Language, however, did present me with problems at the beginning, particularly in group situations. The tendency of Glaswegians to talk fast, coupled with the broad accent, meant that even I had difficulty in understanding some conversations. Only the fact that I was 'adopted' by a drug user in these situations, who took it upon himself to translate, made some of them intelligible.

But no matter how careful one is about the impression given by one's personal appearance, there are other factors (such as mannerisms) which the researcher may not even be aware of but which may limit acceptability, particularly in the early stages of a project. One example will illustrate what I mean.

A conversation with a male drug user began with his remarking how 'well in' I was with the drug users that I knew. I asked him why he thought that was. Amongst other reasons (one being that I appeared to have the attributes of 'a recovering addict', as I seemed to understand the problems of drug users), he referred back to the first evening that I had met him. This was in the drop-in centre, at a meeting held by drug users for drug users which I had been given permission to attend. I had already noted that at this meeting the drug users were provided with tea or coffee in disposable cups, whilst at other meetings in the centre for the families of users, tea was provided in china cups. On this particular evening the leader of the centre was present at the meeting, and proclaimed loudly that the drug users must be given proper cups. My informant recalled this event and said:

The only reason we got those cups was because you were there. He [the leader] thought that because you came from the University that you would have all the social airs and graces and he wanted to impress you. Did you notice the way he crooked his wee finger when he drank his tea? That was to impress you. Well, I watched you and I'd made up my mind that if you did that, then the first time you opened your mouth to speak I'd put you down in such a way that you'd never want to speak to us again.

'And did I?' 'Oh no', he replied, 'and when you did speak you didn't sound like a university researcher at all.' 'So I passed the test?' 'Yes, you passed all the tests.'

Of course, this conversation took place a long way into the fieldwork; I had no way of knowing at the outset how well, if at all, I would be accepted.

Like Irwin (1972), I found that being accepted was not the difficult process that others had led me to believe it would be. Acceptance was not automatic, and different women felt various degrees of suspicion at first. But within a short time of our meeting, most women had developed a large degree of trust in me. It may have been that my sponsor was so well accepted by my informants that his vouching for me was enough to guarantee acceptance. It may have been my topic, as explained to every woman that I met, namely that I was interested in finding out about the issues that were pertinent to women as opposed to men. It may have been that I was not paid for what I was doing (this fact always impressed people when I had occasion to reveal it: 'you mean you only get a measly grant for doing this?'). It may be that in some cases I was seen as a relief from loneliness and boredom. It may simply be that, like Gans, I have 'an honest face, a visible earnestness about wanting to do research, and a quiet demeanour that perhaps tells people that I will not be a threat to them' (Gans, 1982: 57). Whatever the reason, the women I met accepted me into their lives in a way I would not have thought possible at the outset.

Making contact with women drug users, however, was a slow process at first. This was due partly to the fact that there are fewer female than male drug users, and partly to my own fear of rejection. While it appeared that I was trusted by my first couple of contacts, I was not sure to what *extent* they trusted me. I was afraid to be too 'pushy' about asking them to introduce me to other users. My first contacts in the drug centre, then, took the form of informal conversations with the women. It was not difficult for me to listen rather than talk, since at this stage I did not know what questions I wanted to ask. I was afraid, too, about leaving the cosy confines of the centre and venturing onto the streets to further my contacts. Within my first few days, however, I met a woman who took me with her to visit her baby in foster care, took me on a visit to her social worker, and took me shopping for needles and syringes (where I suffered the embarassment of knowing we were being suspected of shoplifting as we picked up and examined the various goods on display).

The study group was eventually obtained by a mix of 'snow-balling' techniques (Morgan-Thomas, 1990; Morrison, 1988; Polsky, 1969) and my almost continuous presence in the area. The snow-balling approach was somewhat modified from the method as generally outlined. Rather than ask to be introduced or given names of others I could contact, when I met a woman I would spend as much time with her as she would allow, participating with her in her daily round, and through this come to meet others in her social circle. My continued presence in the area also led other women drug users to approach me when I was alone, usually asking if I was 'the woman who is interested in women junkies'. In addition, the drug worker in the area would mention my presence and interest to women with whom he came in contact and facilitate introductions where possible. In such ways different groupings were encountered, although all the women in the study knew each other in at least some way.

Becoming accepted and making contacts did not solve all problems. Once contacts began to increase and I moved into the wider community, there arose the problem of what to observe. A single researcher cannot witness all the events in a community, and therefore has to be selective. Schatzman and Strauss have indicated that 'it is important for the field researcher to distinguish between three sets of discrete events: the routine, the special and the untoward' (1973, quoted in Burgess, 1982: 77). I followed this advice, and events I witnessed or took part in ranged from the very routine (sitting around drinking coffee and eating junk food) to accompanying various women on visits to DSS offices or to the HIV clinic; I accompanied them when they were in court, and even went flat-hunting with one woman. I went shopping with some, helping them choose clothes for their children and presents for their friends. I visited them in their homes, rehabilitation centres, and maternity wards, sat with them through withdrawals, watched them using drugs, and accompanied them when they went 'scoring' (buying drugs). I met some of their families and became a visitor in their homes. The only thing I did not do was to join them in their work, shoplifting, prostitution, or whatever. I did once unknowingly, however, walk around the Glasgow Garden Festival with a woman who had shoplifted a couple of jumpers out of a shop on the Festival site and then, again unknowingly, gave her a lift in my car back to where she resold them.

Risks

One aspect of research into the field of criminal involvement distinguishes it from most other areas: the element of risk to the researcher. Risk appears in three forms: legal, health, and personal.

Polsky has argued that 'if one is effectively to study adult criminals in their natural settings he must make the moral decision that in some ways he will break the law himself. He need not be a "participant" observer and commit the criminal act under study, yet he has to witness such acts or be taken into confidence about them and not blow the whistle' (1969: 138). From this, Douglas argued that 'we must try to extend to social scientists the legal protection lawyers and doctors have from being accessories to crimes' (1972: 9).

Twenty years on, no such automatic protection is yet afforded to sociologists. I informed the Drug Squad of my intentions, and was asked to provide a photograph which would help Drug Squad officers identify me and thus avoid the possibility of me being picked up by them. However, the local constabulary refused to circulate a photograph to local police officers. They agreed instead to sign a letter of identification which I carried about with me; but they left me in no doubt that this would offer no immunity if I was found in possession of drugs (including drugs being found in my car), nor would it prevent me from being picked up on the street on suspicion and subjected to a strip search. Once I came perilously close to being picked up. As I was standing with a group of drug users one day, after they had purchased some drugs, we were suddenly accosted by two policemen who simply took hold of the two people closest to them and took them off to the police station. I had been standing next to one of them. Immunity, however, would have hidden from me the feelings experienced in such a situation and denied me the opportunity of showing my informants that I was not a spy. On seeing the expression on my face after this incident, it was quite clear to my companions that, as one said with a laugh, 'that's *one* experience you obviously don't want to have'. Rapport and trust were also fostered the evening I spent tearing around the streets in my car avoiding police because one of my passengers had a warrant out for his arrest. These two incidents were mentioned several times by both female and male users as a way of indicating to others that I was 'all right'.

Staying 'all right' in terms of health is also an issue to be considered by researchers in the drug field. Intravenous drug users do carry infections which should be avoided. AIDS, of course, is the disease which is uppermost in people's minds when they think of intravenous drug users. It is fairly difficult to become infected by the HIV virus; but drug users do carry used needles and they do sometimes bleed, so avoidance of contact is important.

Hepatitis B is common amongst intravenous drug users and is more infectious, particularly in unsanitary conditions. I had been vaccinated against Hepatitis B but, through ignorance, began the course of injections too late and did not know throughout the whole of the fieldwork whether the vaccine was effective. This meant that I had to take precautions where I could throughout this period. Obviously, I could not check up on any of my hostesses' washing up facilities when offered a cup of tea or coffee, and I never refused any such offers. What I was never able to bring myself to do, data or no data, was to engage in the common practice of sharing drinks from a can amongst a group of people. This led to one uncomfortable experience. I accompanied a group of women to the Glasgow Garden Festival on what turned out to be one of the hottest days of the summer. We had purchased some cans to drink—one each—and we had just passed through the Festival gate when one of the women opened hers and passed it around. A couple of the others followed suit and it dawned on me that I was not going to be able to drink mine without sharing it. This I just could not do. So I had to pretend that I was not thirsty and gave my drink to one of the women who promptly shared it out. It was only much later, when we sat at a café and purchased some drinks in glasses, that I was able to quench my thirst!

Other health issues revolve around the stress experienced at points in the research. Doing participant observation is stressful. Continually engaging in conversations which appear 'natural' but in which one is constantly listening with a sociological ear is difficult and mentally exhausting, particularly over long periods of time. By suggesting that the conversations I engaged in were not 'natural', however, I do not mean that the women I spoke to and spent so much time with were in any way deceived or exploited. Like other feminist methodologists, I, too, subscribe to the method whereby the women are treated as 'subjects' rather than 'objects', thus minimizing the gulf between researcher and researched. But it would be naïve to argue that analysis can be achieved without a degree of objectivity. Such objectivity is essential if ongoing analysis (H. Becker, 1970*b*) or grounded theorizing (Glaser and Strauss, 1967), the hallmarks of ethnographic work, are to take place. Only then can important pieces of conversations be seen as confirming hypotheses or suggesting new ones.

Another source of stress in conversations is the constant vigilance required so that confidences are not betrayed. On meeting new women, I always made it clear that what they said to me was confidential and would not be passed on to anyone else. Some information that comes the way of the researcher is common knowledge, however, and can be freely discussed; but it takes time before such occasions can be indulged in with confidence, and this is only possible when the researcher knows enough about the positions that people hold in the community. I made a dreadful mistake one day whilst talking to a group of women. One was a drug user whose children had recently been taken into care by the Social Work Department and we were discussing this. At one point we were joined by a woman new to me. From the way she spoke to the others I assumed that she knew the rest of the group. She asked who I was, and one of the other women told her. On hearing that I was a researcher she wanted more detail. By way of illustration, I said that I was interested in aspects of the lives of women drug users such as them having their children taken into care just like—and I indicated the woman with us. To my horror the new woman turned to her: 'Are you a junkie? Well I may as well tell you that I've got no time for people like you.' I felt angry with myself for exposing this person to such a reaction, and I also felt that my credibility would be utterly destroyed by this incident; but a few days later another member of this group, whom I had not known as a drug user, came to speak to me about her drug use.

Some pieces of information can be difficult for the researcher to cope with. One night one of the women had been beaten up, robbed, and raped when she had gone to buy drugs. She had not told her boyfriend about the rape until the following morning, but even then refused to discuss it with him or seek medical help. He had taken her to the drug worker but, whilst obviously extremely distressed, she also refused to talk to him. When asked if there was anyone she wanted to speak to, she said she would speak to me. By the time I saw her, twenty-four hours had passed since the incident. Once we were left on our own she broke down and told me what had happened, and she finally agreed to go to hospital for the help she needed. I spent almost the whole of the next two days comforting her as she refused to seek professional help, although still in a state of shock.

Another worry which remained with me throughout the fieldwork arose from the illegal nature of much of the information I came across. When given knowledge of a particular illegal activity, be it that someone was 'signing on' and working at the same time or, more exotically, where someone 'stashed kit' I worried that the person in question would be found out and that I, as the outsider, would be suspected of 'grassing.' Drug users, as we will see later in the text, sometimes resort to physical means of exacting justice (they often have no other option) when they feel they have been wronged. Only once did I feel in actual physical danger, from a mentally disturbed drug user who was stabbing people who merely spoke or even looked at him. One morning I was in a building with a woman when another came up to us, looking frightened, and said that 'he' was downstairs and we should leave before anything happened. We had to walk past him to get outside. I was relieved when he was arrested a few days later and eventually given a prison sentence.

During my visit to the police prior to fieldwork, I had been warned in lurid detail of events likely to befall me—I would be mugged, robbed, used as a courier, suspected of dealing. I would be followed and my house would be burgled. None of these things happened. At the end of fieldwork my car still contained its radio and cassette (a source of amazement to the staff at the drop-in centre). However, I did take certain precautions on the basis of the knowledge that drug users *do* steal and rob and, on their own admission, often from people they know and like. I never gave my address to anyone, although they knew the area in which I lived; and, as I wanted to give my telephone number so that I could be contacted at home, I had my number changed to ex-directory to conceal my address.

These precautions were undertaken as much to give my family a degree of protection as myself. The issue of the effect one's research has on one's family is virtually ignored in the literature. Only Weinberg and Williams discuss this at any length (1972: 170). They state that 'the nature of the fieldwork as well as the change in role and self resulting from field experience can affect relationships with persons other than subjects', and later add: 'explaining to one's family ... what one is doing can be awkward and is often settled by obfuscation'.

Quite simply, my family and friends were horrified when it became clear how I *really* planned to carry out my research. Weinberg and Williams argue that 'because of the felt disapprobation certain activities may not be observed, certain places may not be visited'. This is when (I would argue) a degree of obfuscation becomes necessary. Whilst tacitly agreeing on particular no-go areas, as the research proceeded and I became more confident that my family's and friends' concerns were misplaced, I did enter the forbidden areas: I did visit drug users in their homes alone, there were occasions when I was on my own with male drug users and gave them lifts in my car. I was not always totally honest about my activities, although over time, as family members became more relaxed about my safety, I was able to be more open.

Families are also affected in other ways through research of this nature. I had been advised by a worker in the drug field that I should be careful whom I should tell of my actual research plans, as a protection for my children. He knew of cases where the children of those who worked with people who had AIDS or had the HIV virus were shunned by their companions when this became public knowledge. Anxious that this should not happen, particularly to my youngest son, still at primary school, I had not only to be vigilant myself but also to ensure that my children, too, were circumspect in their conversations.

Stress, then, not only arises at the research site but can also spill over into the researcher's personal life. Many of the concerns expressed by my family arose out of their concern for my personal safety, but they also arose from the fact that I am a female.

An Unsuitable Job for a Woman?

A glance through the literature on participant observation studies of inner-city illicit drug users reveals no such studies as having been undertaken by women. Indeed, Rosenbaum, when discussing her methodology for studying female heroin users, states:

although several male ethnographers have done much field work with addicts in urban centres . . . we found that as women we were limited. We felt especially vulnerable, since we were less well equipped to defend ourselves physically than a man. . . . In sum the problems of doing fieldwork in drug communities, the vulnerability of women researchers, the relative secrecy of women addicts and the suspicion aroused by field workers— made us rely much more heavily on our depth interviews in collecting . . . data.   (1981: 147)

The unsuitableness of this type of work for a woman was also pointed out by various people whom I met in the course of this project. A few examples of comments made to me, or in my presence, will illustrate this. They also indicate that women researchers are often viewed first and foremost as women and not as researchers:

This is the brave wee lassie who's venturing into the drug world.   (Drug Squad officer)

It's not a job for a wee lassie like you.   (Police officer)

These streets are no place for a woman on her own.   (Social worker)

You can't possibly intend to work all these nights. What about your family? (Drug worker)

And, seeing me pushing the pram and infant belonging to one of the women:

That's more like it. You look just right behind that pram.   (Staff member of drug centre).

All these comments were made by men. Similar remarks made by male users reflected the conventional view of women prevalent amongst them:

I think you just use this place as an excuse to leave your weans at hame. (Male drug user)

What does your man think about you doing this? If you were mine I'd have you at hame washing the dishes.   (Male drug user)

Shouldn't you be away hame and making your man's tea?   (Male drug user)

It should also be noted, however, that concern for my man's welfare did not prevent them from sexually harassing me!

With the women users, I was invariably asked about my children, although the presence or absence of a partner or his attitude to my work was hardly, if ever, alluded to. Nor did they ever express doubts as to the suitability of my work.

I would argue that what I did is a highly suitable job for a women. I would agree with Wax that 'each gender . . . has its own particular and peculiar advantages' (1979: 514). The fact that I am a woman, I believe, made me more easily accepted and gave me more freedom to explore aspects of the women's lives which a man would have found difficult. Comments from the women themselves confirmed this, especially around issues such as motherhood and relationships with partners. There is, however, very little evidence from the litera-ture to support this contention. McKeganey and Boddy pointed out some of the difficulties experienced in dealing with and being accepted by women drug users in the same area where the present study was carried out (McKeganey and Boddy, 1987). But for the most part, as Wax points out, 'when [men] give us descriptions of how they did their fieldwork they simply do not tell us anything about what happened when they approached women' (1979: 516). I also suspect that the very fact of being female and therefore 'vulner-able', rather than being a drawback, as Rosenbaum argued, instead afforded me a degree of protection and acceptance from the men I encountered which might not have been given to a male researcher.

Rosenbaum also refers to the 'relative secrecy' of women drug users as one reason why fieldwork was less useful than in-depth interviews (Rosenbaum, 1981: 147). Whilst she does not specify in detail what she means by this, it raises one issue in studying drug users which makes participant observation particularly useful. One common stereotype of drug users, both male and female, is that they constantly tell lies. In the body of the text some occasions when this does happen, and the reasons for it, are discussed. Drug users, like most people, want to present a favourable image of themselves, and if this entails lying, or being economical with the truth, they will do this. Moreover, again like other people, there are areas of their lives which they do not want subjected to the scrutiny of strangers. Both these attitudes can mean that they may lie in research situ-ations. As Becker has pointed out, however, presentation of invalid data is easier when the respondent is isolated from her every-day environment, as is the case with other research methodologies, and much more difficult when they are 'enmeshed in social relationships which are important to them ... the opinions and actions of the people they interact with must be taken into account ...All the constraints that affect them in their ordinary lives continue to operate while the observer observes' (H. Becker, 1970c: 46). Participant observation over a lengthy period means not only that the constraints of their everyday environment makes 'faking' (Duelli Klein, 1983: 91) more difficult but also that the presence of the undemanding observer becomes a taken-for-granted part of that environment, again making a false presentation of image and information less likely. One example from fieldwork illustrates this taken-for-granted aspect.

I had recently attended a seminar addressed by an 'expert' in the drug field. During the discussion that followed, someone raised the point that from the presentation it would appear that drug users had fairly high intelligence levels. At this the 'expert' replied: 'I don't think I would say intelligent exactly, more that they have low animal cunning.' The next evening, talking to a group of drug users, I asked for their reaction to this image of them. During the discussion one of them said 'So you really are doing research, you really are taking notes? ... I'd forgotten that.' This occasion, incidentally, also provided an opportunity to show the confidential nature of the data I was gathering. Asked the name of the person who had made the remark about them, I told them that that was impossible: 'after all, you wouldn't like me to name any of you to anybody else.' 'No, that's true. OK, that's cool.'

Towards the end of fieldwork, in order to obtain recordable data, I asked the women if they would consent to talking to me on tape (it is from the transcripts of these interviews that most of the quotations in the body of the text are taken, although there are also some from fieldwork). Ongoing analysis of data throughout fieldwork had revealed the main themes which these interviews would explore. The interviews were unstructured, however, the women being asked if they would 'just tell me all the things we've talked about and discussed since we've met. Perhaps you could start with how you first started using drugs and go on from there.' Only occasionally would I have to introduce one of the themes already identified (and which are the subject of the following chapters). These themes, moreover, were determined by the women themselves. A major aim of this study was to discover the women's views of their world. The issues discussed were those revealed, either through observation or through conversations, both individually and in group situations, as important to the women. Consequently, areas which researchers may be interested in are not covered in depth. AIDS, for example, whilst referred to by the women, did not constitute a major subject of their conversations, and as a result has a very low profile in this study.

Scheduling the interviews, which lasted an average of two to three hours, was extremely difficult. Interviews took place at a time when there was a comparative shortage of drugs. Consequently, asking women to give up three hours when they still had to purchase drugs was next to impossible. Women I had arranged to meet at a particular time would not show up. Altogether, it took four months to complete twenty-six interviews. Ten were comparatively easy, as over this period these women were either in rehabilitation centres or in hospital where I was able to interview them. The remaining sixteen were conducted in the community: in the women's homes; in my car; in the community centre; at the university.

Leaving the Field

During this period I was also aware that another phase of the research was looming—the phase when I would have to take my leave of the women. Like Cannon, I was also aware that I did not want to say 'thank you and goodbye' to them (1989: 74). Some of the women, themselves, expressed disbelief that I would not always be around. In addition, I did not want them to be left with a feeling of having been exploited. However, two events made this stage easier for the women to understand and easier for me to come to terms with.

The interview stage itself meant that I had to disengage from everyday contact in the area. When I returned after some days' absence it was assumed I had been interviewing, and I was asked how successful it had been. Also at this stage my youngest son developed an illness which was to last several months. Having long before reached a stage where the women and I exchanged information and proffered advice to each other about aspects of our lives, including our children, I told them about his illness. After this I was not only continually asked for progress reports on his condition but urged not to come to see them so often if I would rather spend time at home with him. However, I never completely severed my

94-789

connections with the women. I still occasionally pay a visit to the area and talk to any of the women that are there at the time. On these occasions they seem as genuinely pleased to see me as I am to see them, and always ask when the research will be written up and ready to read. I am also still in contact with the drug worker, who keeps me up to date with what is happening in some of the women's lives.

Field research is accompanied by a set of experiences that are, for the most part, unavailable through other forms of social scientific research. These experiences are bound together with satisfactions, embarrassments, challenges, pains, triumphs, ambiguities and agonies all of which blend together into what has been described as the field research adventure. (Shaffir *et al.*, 1980: 17)

I have tried to provide a flavour of what this 'adventure' with drug users is like. What I fear I have not emphasized is the enjoyable aspects of this type of research. I loved doing this type of work; it allowed me insights into the drug using world which I would argue no other method would have revealed.

Profile of the Women

Participant observation brought me into contact with over fifty drug using women. The twenty-six who were eventually interviewed represent the range and variety of ages, drug histories, and social relationships characteristic of the larger group. At any one time, different people are at different stages of their drug using careers. What I tried to do was to include women at these different stages (as the main focus of interest was the lifestyle of women who regarded themselves as established drug users, there are no women at the 'becoming' stage included, although the women I met do reflect on this stage). Accordingly, the women in the study have drug histories ranging from one year to twelve years. They were also at different stages of 'womanhood': some were married; others in steady relationships; some did not have a partner. Some had children; some did not; some were single parents, some gave birth to children during the period of observation, some became pregnant.

The group, however, should not and cannot be considered representative in any statistical sense. Participant observation is not intended to produce a representative sample (Plant and Reeves, 1976). There are two reasons, moreover, why a representative group of female drug users would be difficult, if not impossible, to obtain. First, neither the size of the overall female drug using population in Glasgow nor the size of that population in the inner-city area in which I observed the women was known at the time the research was carried out.[4] Second, there was no information available on the demographic characteristics of female drug users in the area: average age, average length of time of drug use, and so on. However, although no 'objective' or 'scientific' assessment can be made of the representativeness of the women studied, my time spent with the women has made me confident that they are characteristic of the variety of female drug users in their part of the city.

The demographic characteristics of the twenty-six women are outlined below. Names and some demographic details of individual women have been changed to preserve anonymity. Moreover, where particular incidents may possibly still identify some women, they have been assigned pseudonyms which apply to those specific incidents only, thus ensuring that they will not be associated with other statements made by them in other parts of the text.

The mean age of the women was twenty-four years, and the range was from seventeen to thirty-four years. The mean length of time the women had been using drugs intravenously was five years, varying between one and twelve years. Between them the women had a total of twenty-six children, three of them born during field-work. Three women were pregnant at the end of fieldwork. The ages of the children ranged from newborn to seventeen years. Four of the women were childless. Fifteen of the children were looked after by their mothers, although three were removed into care during fieldwork. Ten of the others were looked after by other family members, mostly grandparents. Four of the women were married. Eleven others, including two who had been divorced, were in steady relationships.

The area in which the women lived was characterized by high rates of unemployment. At the beginning of the year in which most

---

[4] Haw (1985) estimated that there were 5,000 intravenous drug users in Glasgow at the end of 1983. The ratio of male to female varied between the different data sets upon which the estimate was based, and ranged from 5 : 1 to 2 : 1. A study by Frischer (1992), undertaken after fieldwork for this study was completed, estimated that there were 9,424 intravenous drug users in Glasgow in 1989. The ratio of male to female was estimated as 2.6 : 1.

of the fieldwork was carried out, 23 per cent of the population were registered as unemployed as opposed to 19.6 per cent in the city as a whole. Youth unemployment was even higher: 30.7 per cent were registerd as unemployed against 27.3 per cent overall in the city. Fifty-one per cent of all who were registered as unemployed had been unemployed for more than one year, again a rate higher than the overall city average of 48.5 per cent (Glasgow District Council, 1988). This pattern was more pronounced in the women studied. Only one had employment during my observation period, and that was in the informal economy. One other woman obtained a job as a cleaner for six weeks. Seven of the women had never had a job. The kind of work that other women had had in the past had all been low-skill, low-paid jobs in service or manufacturing industries, such as waitressing, shopkeeping, and machine operation.

Organization and Style of Presentation

The chapters are organized around the themes associated with a typical drug using career. In Chapter 2, the women reflect on how they first became involved in drug use and how they came to re-cognize themselves as dependent on drugs. Chapter 3 focuses on the activities directly related to maintaining their drug use, and introduces two essential elements associated with this: 'scoring' and 'grafting'. Chapter 4 begins to explore the wider aspects of their lifestyle, looking at the women's social networks and the effect drug use has on these. It is in this chapter and the next, which concentrates on the women as mothers, that the blend of ordinary concerns and deviant activities which characterizes the women's lives becomes apparent. Chapter 5, on mothering, also provides an account of the women's views of the attitudes of social service pro-viders towards female drug users. Chapter 6 explores the women's disillusionment with their lifestyle and their varying efforts to change the patterns of their lives. The concluding chapter draws together the findings and explores the implications.

Struck by the eloquence and insight of much of what was said, I have used extensive quotations from the women in the style of speech used by them. The Glaswegian dialect used by the women may be unfamiliar to some readers; for those words or expressions which are peculiarly Glaswegian or Scottish, a glossary is provided.

Translation into 'standard English' would have meant that the tone, intensity, and sincerity of what the women had to say would have been lost. During my period spent in the area, drug users (male as well as female) had much to say about non-drug users, including researchers, who had the audacity to 'tell us all about ourselves' and the presumption to discuss and debate their situations in an atmosphere, as the drug users saw it, of ignorance of what it was 'really like' to be a drug user. With this in mind, I have tried to represent their views as faithfully as possible.

2

Starting Off

Drug using careers, like any others, have a starting-point at which the novice enters and begins a process of learning the skills necessary to achieve the status of a competent member. This chapter focuses on this process, from the women's first encounters with illicit substances, following their progress up to the point where they perceived themselves as addicted. The women recollect how they were introduced to drug taking, their move to 'hard' drugs, and their subsequent move to injecting. The women's own active involvement at each stage becomes apparent, and the stereotypical image of women drug users as 'passive victims' is thus refuted.

Routes into Drug Use

For an individual to engage in drug use, as in any other activity, the opportunity to participate must be available. A finding similar to those of other studies (Binion, 1982; Chein *et al.*, 1964; Cuskey, 1982; Eldred and Washington, 1976; Gerstein *et al.*, 1979; Kaufman, 1985; Marsh, 1982; Marsh and Simpson, 1986; Parker *et al.*, 1988; Prather, 1981; Reed, 1985; Rosenbaum, 1981; Silverman, 1982; Suffet and Brotman, 1976; Waldorf, 1973) was that, for all the women, the availability and use of drugs within their social circles facilitated the beginning of their drug use.

Well like here every second person you know must be into something . . . you are bound to wonder 'Is it good or no?'. . . it would be different if you stayed in a place where there are only about one or two people in the whole place using.   (Rose)

Whilst there is general agreement in the recent literature that social networks, as opposed to 'evil pushers' (Parker *et al.*, 1988; Pearson, 1987*a*; Pearson *et al.*, 1986) or iatrogenic use, facilitate entry to drug use for females, there is disagreement over the composition of such networks. The majority view is that women are mainly introduced to drug use by males (Binion, 1982; Eldred and Washington, 1976; Gerstein *et al.*, 1979; Prather, 1981; Reed, 1985; Silverman, 1982; Suffet and Brotman, 1976; Waldorf, 1973), or that the addicted male associate is the greatest predisposing factor for female drug use (Cuskey, 1982). Chein *et al.* (1982), on the other hand, found that only a minority of women in their study were first introduced to heroin by a male user. Others have shown that different factors have to be taken into account when considering male associates as a predisposing factor. Parker *et al.* (1988) found that women in their study who had come into treatment were more likely to have been introduced to heroin through a male user, but that those who had not sought treatment were more likely to have been introduced by their female peers. Kaufman (1985) and Rosenbaum (1981) both found that women over the age of twenty-five were more likely to have been introduced and to continue drug use through association with a male drug using partner, but that younger women were more likely to have begun through female friends.

The findings of this present study show that both female and male friends were instrumental in introducing the women to drug use. Some women claimed that they began using drugs because 'everyone' within their peer group was doing so; others began in a more select group: their 'pals'; whilst other women first became involved through a more exclusive relationship with a boyfriend.

Everybody Uses

Everybody was just smoking hash . . . well I didn't like drink and someone would say 'Well I smoke hash, have you ever tried a wee bit of hash?' 'Oh no, so give us a bit and I'll try it' and that was the way I got into it. Everybody all sitting smoking hash.   (Lorraine)

I got into acid at school. Everybody did that.   (Rose)

I just wanted to be one of the crowd.   (Michelle)

Using with Pals

I started smoking dope. My brother used to smoke dope with his pals and I just used to steal wee bits off him when I was thirteen. And my pal and I used to dog school [play truant] and we got one of they wee cigarette machines. All we used to do was fall asleep and wake two hours later. And then when I was about fourteen or something, I had a pal, she had just got a job in a chemist's shop. And she was a clever lassie and the pharmacist was into training her and that. She was only supposed to be on the till and selling deodorant and things, but he took her into the back of the shop, trying to teach her so she could be a pharmacist sort of thing. And she was coming out every night with different tablets.   (Sharon)

It was just one of the lassies brought them into school, knocked them [tranquillisers] off her mother. And of course the guinea pig, I said, 'Oh here I'll try them' and I liked them.   (Louise)

I started taking DFs, me and Cathy . . . my boyfriend, Tommy, he used to take heroin all the time and he got the jail and I started hanging about with Cathy, and this guy started selling Difs. At this time it was £1 for ten DFs, now its £4 for ten. And Cathy was going, 'Come on and we'll get the DF things', and I said, 'What do they do to you?' She went, 'Just make you full of it' and I went, 'Why not?' So we went and got ten each and we took them and all I did all night was be sick everywhere. And I thought, 'I hate these things, they're horrible'. But after the sickness went away, I started feeling that I could do anything and dead itchy . . . and I had seen Tommy doing that . . . so the next night we got them again and then we started getting them every time we had money and then it was every day.   (Helen)

Two points of interest arise from Helen's recollections. First, although she had a drug user as a partner, he had not been directly instrumental in her initial drug use. Second, contrary to the findings of other studies which suggest that women seldom encourage other women to become users (Polit *et al.*, 1976), it was her friend who cajoled her into her first use. This was, moreover, the dominant pattern amongst the women in this study. First use of at least 'quasi-licit' drugs (Prather, 1981: 733) was more likely to take place with and through other females rather than males.

Boyfriends

Association with male drug using partners was, however, instrumental in other important ways. In particular, rather than being the first to introduce the women to drug use in general, a more common role for male partners was for them to be implicated in the move from 'soft' to 'harder' substances.

The Move to Hard Drugs

Male partners could be involved in the women's move to 'hard' drugs in three ways. First, male partners could directly introduce the women to such substances:

Well I was staying with a guy and it was more or less through him that I got into drugs. I was in a homeless unit and I met him when I was in there. And I was experimenting with them. He was bringing me up tems and I was snorting them, buying DFs, jellies, you know just daft things. I never touched smack at that time, then I got my own hoose and he was in the jail and when he came oot he came and stayed with me and that's when all the jaggin' started and it just went from bad to worse then.   (Louise)

I was full of drink and hash and I was staying with this lassie at the time and she was going oot with a boy and I was going oot with his pal and she was wanting to go down and see them, but I didn't. It was my birthday and I was wanting to go to the dancing—and she's like that, 'Och, come on'. So I went and when we got there they had opened this poke and there was smack in it, but we didnae even know what the word smack was . . . I was like that, 'Smack, what's smack?' and they're saying, 'Heroin'. I had never even read it in the paper or heard it on the telly or anything like that. (Michelle)

Partners could also make such substances easily available or socially acceptable to the women (Parker *et al.*, 1988):

I was sixteen and I was just taking dope for a while. And then I ended up going out with a dealer. And he was dealing smack, and I started off by taking you know like a tenner bag a day.   (Alice)

I don't think . . . if it hadn't been for the fact that Des had tried then I maybe wouldn't have. But because he had tried it and he looked healthy and at the time I was all starry eyed about him, I tried it.   (Rose)

Third, and perhaps most importantly, male partners acted as a role model from which the women learned the skills and knowledge required to purchase, use, and recognize physical effects. Helen has already demonstrated this in her recollection of the first time she used dihydrocodeine. She had been able correctly to interpret the itching feeling she had felt as part of the effect of the drug because of her previous observation of her boyfriend's behaviour. His influence was also apparent in her reminiscence of her first time with heroin:

One day, I couldnae get any DFs, the guy I got them from got caught selling them. I said to my pal, 'Come and we'll get a tenner bag?' She said, 'Aye. But where do we get it from?' I said 'We go down the road and get it off Brian, that's what my boyfriend does. But listen, see when we get down there don't act as if you don't know what you're talking about. If they think we're just two daft lassies they'll just rip us off.'

So we went away doon and Brian was standing there. I saw a few people come up and say his name and ask for kit. So I went up to him, 'Any kit, any smack?' and he went, 'What are you looking for?' 'A tenner bag.' He was just going to give us it. But I said, 'Want to show us it?' He opened it up and showed us it. I had seen it before because of my boyfriend. I knew what it was like and said, 'That's brand new' but my pal went 'Whit! There's no danger of me paying a tenner for that. A tenner? No way.' I went, 'Lisa, shut up'. You see, Avril, they were going to realise that we didn't know what we were into if we did that. But she said again, 'I'm no paying for that, Helen.' I went, 'Shut up Lisa. That's brand new Brian, give us it.'

We walked along the road and I went, 'Lisa, what did you expect to see just now?' She said, 'A right big bag'. I said, 'Don't talk crap, that would cost millions of pounds'—she was thinking about the ones see on the telly, that've got caught. She went, 'No danger Helen, we've just been ripped off'. I said, 'I'm telling you Lisa, that's it. I've seen Tommy getting it.'

So we went along to my house and we've locked the door. So we start, 'Right what do we do—we put it on an LP and chop it out'. So we chopped it out. I said to Lisa, 'Right, we half it now, and now we roll up a coupon and just put the coupon up your nose and now go along the line and snort it.' So we've halved it, right, and I've done that, 'Right you take that one Lisa, 'cause that's the biggest'. I was giving her the biggest—I would never do that now, you know what I mean? The two of us were scared in case we were going to overdose. And she was like that, 'No, no way, you take it', and I was like that, 'No'. So we ended up tossing a coin to see who was getting the biggest. We tossed and tossed the coin to see who was getting the wee-est. So I ended up losing so I had to take the biggest. 'Cause you never get them exactly right, Avril. So I snorted mine and she snorted hers and we were sitting on the bed—and it was horrible by the way you know—and next minute—it feels like—see when you've snorted, it feels like tickly and a wee bit nippy—so I thought—I was like that, 'This isn't coming on me', you know after a couple of minutes. Lisa's like that, 'Neither's mine'. So I've done that, you know sniffed my nose and the next minute it has all come down my throat. You can taste it. And that's when you know you're going to start feeling it—you know once you taste it. I didn't know that. It was just hanging in my nose sort of thing. It was just in my nose, so I tasted it—I was like that, 'Oh no, I feel sick'. But eventually I swallowed it and she's done it as well and then a few minutes later the two of us have started feeling all warm. She and I were like that, 'This is excellent', and she was like that, 'Aye this is brilliant, you know'. We went away oot for a walk. It was snowing and everything and we're walking aboot with no jackets on or nothing 'cause it makes you feel dead warm. We were walking about, 'This is brilliant'. And the next night we got it again.

Helen's vivid recollection of the first time she purchased and used heroin acutely demonstrates her boyfriend's influence in her acquiring the skills involved in becoming a successful drug user: knowledge of where to purchase drugs; who to buy from; what to say; what to do with them. However, despite the influence of her male partner in acquiring such skills, she also demonstrates her own active involvement in her use of heroin.

Boyfriends may have been important facilitators in the ways we have seen: introducing some women to heroin, making it easily available, and indirectly showing the necessary skills; but in no cases did the women fit the model of passive victim, the women themselves firmly rejecting such a status:

A lot of people think it was Simon that persuaded me into using but it wasn't. I used to see the states that he got into and I wanted to try it. I've always been like that, I cannae see green cheese.   (Fiona)

Indeed, many of the women began using substances in spite of their partners' disapproval.[1] For the most part the women, like the drug users in Pearson's study (1987a), put the 'blame' firmly on themselves:

I mean all my pals and people I knew didnae take drugs. And then when I went out with David he and his pals were all taking heroin and I just wanted to try it . . . But I couldnae blame David, because he wasnae there when I took it.   (Sandra)

I never, ever, blame anybody for what I've done. If you don't want to take something there is no way you will take it.   (Alice)

Explaining the Move to Hard Drugs

Like drug users observed in recent studies, all the women were polydrug users (Hammersley *et al.*, 1990a; Klee *et al.*, 1990; Sakol *et*

---

[1] For similar findings, see Rosenbaum (1981).

al., 1989). Their preferred substances were heroin, buprenorphine,[2] temazepam, and dihydrocodeine,[3] depending to a large extent on availability. Although initial use of these substances was usually confined to swallowing or snorting, most of the women regarded their first encounter with these substances as another dimension in their drug using lives, many of them referring to it as how they 'really' began using drugs despite having had earlier experiences of drug taking. Indeed, when recalling earlier use it was clear that, for many of the women, this was regarded as something that was commonplace.[4] As Lorraine said: 'It would just be like you taking a glass of Lambrusco'.

Whilst in retrospect the women regarded their move to heroin and these other substances as different from their previous encounters with drugs, when explaining why they had made this change they gave reasons similar to those for earlier encounters with drugs: they were tried out of curiosity, because they were available, and because they were used in the women's social circles.

And then it must have been the sort of thing to do, to get into smack. (Rose)

And then from there it was smack. That was the next thing to try and all. (Sharon)

It just grew, all of us, right round about the same age. One started and then their pals started and then another lot started and it just ended up most of us were more or less using. (Donna)

Yet some did recall that they had been aware of heroin's awesome reputation, and that this had influenced their first encounter with it. Helen has already told us how neither she nor her friend wanted the largest share of their first purchase. Sharon was even more cautious:

The first time I got heroin I was right ... [*indicating wariness*] —about doing it. I had a friend and she got some smack and there must have been eight crackin' deals in it. And we walked aboot with it all night. We knew ... they say heroin kills and all that, you know? We didnae know what

[2] For similar findings, see Hammersley, Lavelle, and Forsyth (1990), Morrison (1989), O'Connor *et al.* (1988), Robertson (1987), Sakol *et al.* (1989).

[3] For similar findings on temazepam, see Chowdhury and Chowdhury (1990), Klee *et al.* (1990). For similar findings on dihydrocodeine, see Swadi *et al.* (1990).

[4] For similar findings, see McKeganey and Boddy (1987).

to dae with it. So goin' home that night we threw it away over a scrap-
yard wall. When I think aboot that now!   (Sharon)

Whilst Sharon, like all the women in this study, did progress to
heroin, recreational use of less potent substances did not inevitably
lead to experimentation with more serious forms of drug taking.
The women spoke of friends and peers who had been involved in
earlier experimentation with them but who did not go on to use
'hard' drugs. When speaking of such friends, they also revealed
what has been found in previous studies of female users, namely the
negative effect such drug use can have on women's self esteem
(Christenson and Swanson, 1974; Dorn and South, 1985; Rosenbaum,
1981). Not for them the image of the 'stand up cat' (Feldman, 1968:
137). When Michelle told me that she had first started experimenting with drugs because it was what everyone at school was
doing, she continued:

The first time I used it I got the giggles and all that and it was dead
brilliant and then I was taking downers and drink and acid and all that.
Going into school and having a pure scream at the teachers. Like that,
'Michelle, what are you doing? You're doing everything all wrong.' And
everybody's all—they're no' laughin' at you, they're laughin' *with* you at the
time but noo they're laughing at you the ones that arenae junkies noo.
They'll go like that, 'Crackpot—I knew she'd end up like that'.

And Sharon, whose friend had stolen drugs from the chemist shop,
spoke of her:

She was the smart one. She would maybe take one now and again and she
was neither up nor down. Oh no. But me and my other pals . . . It was curiosity . . . a few lassies. And some are alright now but some are junkies and
in the jail.

Of course, these comments were made in retrospect and may not
accurately reflect how the women had felt at the time. Some of
those whose drug use has become problematic are apt to forget the
'joys' of drug use (Pearson, 1987*a*; Rosenbaum, 1981).

    Some women expressed surprise at their use of heroin because
they had previously held strong opinions about its use:

At first when I found out that my pal was doing it I was like that, 'That's
terrible, you're Catholics, you shouldnae be doing that', that's how strongly
I was against it. But one night somebody asked me for £7.00, they were
short of £7.00 to get half a gram—that was £40.00. There were about four

or five of them into it but at that time half a gram went a long way, the quality of it was a lot better. And they said they would give me the £7.00 worth for it. You know £7.00 was a lot, and I don't know why but I just took it and I liked it. It made me sick but I liked the feeling. It was an excellent feeling and it just graduated from there.   (Kate)

Avril, I was one of them that kept saying 'What do you take that stuff for?' He was so good and happy and everything without it, but see the minute he'd take it he completely changed. It was like Jekyll and Hyde. He was a totally different person, dead moany and sometimes he would never come up to the hoose for two days and I would be sitting there . . . 'cause I knew he was using I was like that, 'He's deid'. I'd be away doon the hospitals and everything . . . looking oot my window all the time. He just made my life hell when he was using . . . See when I started using, everybody was like that to me 'Helen, you're the last person we thought would have been using', 'cause of the way I used to talk about Tommy.   (Helen)

Well it was . . . I was goin' about with John since I was thirteen and I'm now twenty, and I mean he was all . . . all his pals were drug users, right. I just never touched anything, I never took anything. I was always against it. I was always arguing with him. He'd come in full of it and I would argue with him and it would take his stone away, so we used to always fall out, you know. And then it was just up until about fifteen months ago and I went and fell out with him and I just started using myself. But it was tems. And that was it. He was in the jail. But I don't know what it was, 'cause it wasn't curiosity, I know that. I just don't know what it was.   (Vicky).

Just as the use of soft drugs did not always inevitably lead to more serious involvement, neither was such use a necessary precondition for use of hard drugs. A few women had begun by using heroin straightaway. For such women, their initial drug use had a more directly functional role:

Well when my father died I was upset and I was drinking heavily at the time. One of my pals said that heroin would be better for me as alcohol just makes you more depressed. So I tried it and she was right, it did make me feel better.   (Joanne)

It was postnatal depression that started me. When I first met Donnie he used to say to me, 'Going to watch this for me?'—you know, his works— 'I'm a diabetic'. So I used to take it in like a right idiot 'cause I didn't know anything about drugs before I met him . . . I didn't even know what they were all sitting there asleep for. I was that daft. So I used to watch them. I used to think he was a diabetic and all the rest of it and then he started selling it when we got a house, you know to get stuff for the house. So I had drugs in the house. So after I had the baby I had this postnatal depression and the doctor didnae give me anything for it. And then one day, no' long after I had come oot frae the hospital, Donnie said to me 'Going to stash this for me?' So I went, 'Aye'. So he was watching the baby and I'm down the stairs and I just took a big lump oot of it myself to see what it would be like. And it was brilliant! It was snowing that night and I went away out for a walk with the pram and the wean. I just wanted to get out, 'cause when you take it at first you are all jumping about. It's great at first.   (Judy)

After I had my wee lassie I suffered postnatal depression and all that and my doctor said I was too young to get treated for it because I was only seventeen so she just sent me hame and it just got worse and worse and worse and I used to sit in the hoose greetin' all the time. And then one night he came in full of it and he says, 'I've got a couple of tems here for you'. At first I said I didnae want them, but he said they would make me feel better. And it did, it lifted my depression . . . I still say that had I never suffered with the depression I would never have started. All these years I had been going with my boyfriend and I never touched it and I knew he was taking it and I still despised—I hated him for being a junkie and I hated all junkies. I hated the word, I hated the thought of a needle breaking my skin but it was just pure depression 'cause after that first hit it made me feel good and I just continued taking them.   (Diane)

The evidence presented thus far cautions against the search for one overriding factor which can explain entry into illicit drug use. The futility of such a search was neatly summed up by Rose:

Some people get into it through boredom, through despair about what life is about; some people get into it for excitement. There's too many ways, too wide a spectrum of people.

But what is also apparent from the women's recollections is the attractions of drug use, seen in their expressions of 'brilliant', 'excellent', when describing their first encounters. Many talked of heroin making them sick the first time they used it, but even when this happened, the good feelings were still paramount:

The first time I tried it, it made me as sick as a dog. It was crazy. I remember Brian was like that 'You alright? You sure you're OK?' I was like that, hanging over the toilet seat spewing, 'Aye, this is brilliant'.   (Rose)

I remember my first hit so well because it was my sixteenth birthday. I felt . . . it's a feeling you cannae explain. I was burlin', it was like floating on a cloud. I was really sick, but the sicker you are at the beginning the higher you get. I remember I slid right down the wall and the guy that gave me the hit said, 'How do you feel?' 'Brilliant' as I slid right down.   (Michelle)

Many women discovered that the euphoric effects, whilst important, were not the only attractions attached to drug use. For some it expanded their social options[5] by providing a more exciting lifestyle or increasing their self-confidence:[6]

I just thought it was exciting and daring. Maybe if I had met a guy that was into something exciting and daring in another way it would have been totally different. Do you know what I mean? I think there was always this wee bit in me that wanted to do something exciting.   (Rose)

At first you think it is great. You are in with everybody and all that and you want to be with everybody, know what I mean? . . . Aye, oh it was magic at first. Aye. These were all big drug dealers and you thought you were great. Going about with all the people that everybody knew, it was a new thing for me and I loved it at the time . . . I had just started to take drugs at the time and I thought it was all magic.   (Jenny)

Like I could talk to people, I'd just ramble on when I shouldn't. But it wouldnae bother me, cause you don't get embarrassed, because you're so stoned anyway.   (Susan)

Since I started using drugs, it was always, 'Oh no, no, this isn't for me being straight'. You need pals round about you. That is how I looked at it. I had always felt dead lonely and dead left out. I always wanted people round about me, and junkies are always there . . . it never made me be dead lonely because there were always junkies about . . . You see I had always kept myself to myself. So people always running about me was fascinating . . . I was dead shy, dead embarrassed, everything like that. But once you are full of it, you don't really care. 'Cause you have got a false face on. It's dead different, you are dead false and kid on to everybody, big bravy and all that, and you are not really. But that is how you come across to everybody. (Emma)

These pleasurable and beneficial aspects were the spur to continued drug taking; but to maintain them, sooner or later a common development occurred — switching to intravenous use.

Move to Injecting

The major reason for the switch to injecting was that it was more economical. With all the used substances, tolerance develops. A

---

[5] For similar findings, see Rosenbaum (1981).
[6] For similar findings, see Jeffries (1983), Wolfson and Murray (1986).

larger amount of the substance is required to produce the same effect, and this of course makes drug use more expensive. Injecting is the fastest route by which substances reach the brain, and drugs arrive there in a purer, less diluted state than is the case with smoking or snorting. This results in two factors of interest to the drug user. A more intense effect (known as a 'rush') is experienced. It also means that more of an effect can be obtained with a similar amount taken in other ways, or that the same effect is achieved with less. This has obvious economic implications.

I started smoking the smack. I was on that for a wee while and then it was getting too expensive, so I started hitting it, so it'd be cheaper . . . and you get a rush . . . Eh, aye it's different. You get a rush and it hits you faster. (Susan)

I needed to start taking hits because I was snorting too much. I could hit a third of what I was snorting and it would save money.   (Helen)

In much of the earlier literature on drug use the move to injecting is portrayed as a symbolic act which drug users see as the event which signifies their progression from mere drug user to that of addict or junkie (Alksne *et al.*, 1967; Rosenbaum, 1981). More recent studies argue that such symbolism changes from area to area (ISDD, 1987). Certainly, the women in this study, whilst making a sharp qualitative distinction between use of injectable and non-injected drugs when recalling their earlier drug use, did not necessarily associate injecting with addict status. Within the women's culture, intravenous drug use was so common that they did not necessarily see the change to injecting as signalling a change in their status.

Successful intravenous drug use involves learning certain skills. The user has to learn injecting techniques: how to find a vein, how to operate a syringe. She also has to learn how to prepare drugs for injection. Powder, which is the form in which heroin is purchased, cannot be injected. It has to be made soluble. The impurities found in most street heroin—brick dust, talcum powder, and the like—have to be filtered out as far as possible in order to minimise the amount of harm that these can cause when injected into the bloodstream. These skills are rarely possessed by novice intravenous users. Until they have been developed (and this can take some time, and in some instances never happens (Howard and

Borges, 1970; Rosenbaum, 1981)), a more experienced user has to be found who will administer the injection. For some of the women, this was their male partner:

I got Des to inject me because I couldn't inject myself for years.   (Rose)

I started hitting up and he injected it for me.   (Emma)

In some cases male partners had no objection to performing this task. Emma spoke of her partner as being glad to do it for her:

He thought it was great, somebody else using with him.

With other partners, initial reluctance had to be overcome. For Helen's partner, economic reasoning fell on deaf ears and he had to be appealed to on other grounds.

He said, 'No, Helen, I don't want you to start hitting'. I said, 'Look, I'm no' getting a stone any mair, I just feel alright . . . I want a stone'. And he went, 'Right, I'll give you a hit then'.

Louise explained her own partner's negative reaction in terms of a moral code that existed among drug users:

He wouldn't give me a hit. If we bought kit on my giro day or his I'd have to snort it. He wouldn't give me a hit . . . He just used to say to me, 'I'm no' giving you your first hit, get yourself another daftie to do it but it's no' going to be me' . . . I think for any junkie to give anyone who isn't a junkie their first hit, it isnae, it's no' something I would dae having been through the drug scene, I couldnae give someone their first hit. I mean it wouldnae be right because I mean it would seem as if you . . . I mean the stone's brilliant, see when you have your first hit, it's excellent, so if you are giving them their first hit and they're experiencing it by injecting it, saying that's brilliant, well they're gonnae go and do it again. So you're going to feel that it's your fault, if they end up junkied up and in a heavy state and in the jail, you're gonnae feel guilty, that's the way I would feel anyway. And a lot of people feel that way that I know so I suppose that's how he must have felt.

The shared existence of such a moral code is questionable, however, and was perhaps the product of wishful thinking by Louise, who by the time I met her was regretting her drug use. Because the fact remained that she and all the women managed, without much difficulty, to find someone to give them their first hit. When male partners either failed them or were not available, friends usually performed the requested deed. Louise continued:

So what I did, I got someone else to do it. It was my pal, a lassie I've known for years. She's a junkie so she gave me my first hit. And he cracked up, because he'd found out I'd had a hit, but I mean, I went out the next day and bought two tenner bags and gave him one and I had the other and says to him, 'Gie me a hit', and he never said, 'No', he said, 'Aye, alright'. So he couldnae have been that bothered.   (Louise)

Indeed, other women said that they had had no difficulty in finding someone willing to give them their first injection:

It was my pal, and she was a junkie, who gave me my first hit . . . she wasnae bothered.   (Judy)

The first intravenous use does not usually provide enough experience for consequent injections to be carried out by that individual. A continual source of injectors has therefore to be found if the experience is to be repeated. But some of the disadvantages involved in this practice sooner or later become apparent, making the move to self-administration sensible and rational.

Being injected by others can be a costly exercise, requiring payment in the form of drugs. Sometimes injectors can also defraud their 'clients':

My wee sister's boyfriend, he used to gie me a hit . . . well, if I would buy him a tem, a bit of kit for a hit, he would gie me it. But when I only had enough for myself but nothing for him it would be, 'Oh I cannae' and I would get left to rattle . . . he wouldnae even gie me it . . . well he did once, but he gied me water. I was ragin'. I had got a bit of kit. And we went over to his hoose. And I didnae . . . I knew . . . I've seen people like making it up and all that, but I didnae really want to dae it myself in case I made an arse of it, and . . . this day I was really no' well, 'cause I had been on kit, and then I went on to tems, because I couldnae get kit, and it just gied me a sore stomach and sore heid. And it made me right bad. And then I scored kit. So I went over to his hoose to get a hit, and he went and fixed it up for me, and gied me water, with a wee tint of kit in it. And I knew, I knew in myself, you know, but . . . 'cause I wouldnae gie him a bit 'cause I was right bad. And I had took the shakes and all that, and then . . . he gied me water. And I was ragin', cause it didnae square me up or nothin'. And then I pulled him up about it, but he denied it. There was nothing much I could dae, but I soon learnt how to dae it myself after that.

A second risk is that the injector may not be competent:

I always needed Tommy to give me a hit and it wasnae until one day he wasnae there and this guy said he'd give me a hit . . . so I set mine up and he set his up and he done that, 'Right Helen I'll give you a hit in a minute once I get myself'. He hadnae been using that long. So I was sitting watching him and he was like that—blood everywhere. And I went, 'Ah no, he's a butcher, no danger'. So I was just sitting there and I had a tie round my arm and I pulled my sleeve up and I seen the vein sticking right out and I just done that, stuck it in and I pulled it back and the blood all came into it and see because I had done it myself, I felt brilliant. See just seeing the blood all coming into it I felt dead proud as if it was something dead crackin' I had done or something. I put it in myself, you know. From then on I just started hitting myself so I did.   (Helen)

Unlike the women in Rosenbaum's study (1981), who found this a frightening move which removed more control from their lives, the feeling of pride expressed by Helen was a common reaction:

I became a pure expert . . . a lot of skill.   (Sharon)

In a group of women whose life chances had provided little of which to be proud, this sense of achievement attached to their use of drugs should not be underestimated as a way of binding them further to such use.

Recognition of Addiction

Moving to intravenous drug use was not, as we have seen, evidence of a status passage, but regarded as a necessary development if the benefits of drug taking were to be continued and costs were to be kept to a minimum. Although at this stage the women all knew many within their community who were regarded as 'junkies', injection of drugs was not a sufficient factor in definition. Physical withdrawal symptoms when drug use ceased, or the inability to find a suitable vein, were the factors by which most woman realised they had reached the state of being a 'junkie'.

Regular use of opiates produces physical dependence, such dependence being affected by factors such as the amount and period used. When use is withdrawn, the body responds with a set of symptoms which were described as similar to those experienced during a bout of influenza:

At first I thought I had the cold because I had all these sore heads and you've got sort of cold symptoms. You've got sore head, runny nose, sneezes, your eyes all watery, you yawn all the time, your legs get sore, belly,

your arms and you really feel as if you have the 'flu. You don't feel like
eating and it can cause you to be sick and you've got a sore stomach. Well
that's the way it is.   (Laura)

In addition sleeplessness is a problem, as well as a feeling of rest-
lessness:

I couldnae get to sleep. I was lying in my bed and my legs were all jumpy
and everything and my back was all sore.   (Helen)

But such symptoms did not immediately provoke a recognition
of physical dependence. This association had to be learned, and was
recognised only when other, more experienced users pointed it out
(Dai, 1937; Lindesmith, 1968; Rubington, 1967). Helen continued:

And he went, 'You've been using, haven't you?' I said, 'No, what are you
talking about?' and he's like that, 'You have. What have you been taking?' I
says, 'I've just been taking DFs'. He said, 'No you've no' cause you're
strung oot'. I said 'What's strung oot?' I didnae even know what it meant,
Avril. And he says, 'It means that your body's got that used to taking these
tablets and noo you've no' got any, your body is wanting them'. I said,
'Don't talk crap, you hear of that on the telly'. 'I'm telling you Helen, you're
strung oot. Are you're legs all jumpy and you cannae keep them at peace? It
feels as if you are itchy inside your skin but you cannae get to it?' And I
says, 'Aye'. 'Well I'm telling you that's how you're strung oot.'

It was at this stage, for most, that they realized that they were no
longer simply drug users, but were now addicted:

And I didn't realise and then after a while I was telling someone and they
were saying, 'Where is it . . . it's not the cold and it's not the 'flu, you've
been taking difs too long and you've got immune to them and it's getting to
the stage where you are getting strung oot for them and you're going to
have to keep adding mair on until you feel that wee bit better'. And that's
what happened. I was addicted to them and I had to get them all the time.
(Laura)

I was strung oot and I thought I had the 'flu and I was lying on the couch
and this guy said to me, you know the guy that gave me my first hit, 'You're
strung oot' and I'm saying 'I'm no' strung oot, I'm no' addicted and all
that'. And then it wasnae until I really thought about it and he said, 'Are you
no'? Here, have another hit'. Gave me a hit and I felt brand new and that's
when I knew that I was addicted.   (Michelle)

I woke up one morning and I felt ill. So I was saying to this lassie I knew, I
says to her, 'I feel terrible'. She went, 'You're strung oot, Judy'. And see

when she said to me I *was* strung out, I *was* strung out, you know, in the head. Soon as somebody says to you, 'You're strung out', that's you, you've got it . . . I didn't know until she said to me. I just thought it was the cold. That's what it felt like, running nose and everything. And then, 'Oh, I'll need to get it'. You know that's what I kept saying to myself. So that is how it started with me.   (Judy)

Most women had come to this recognition when, for one reason or another, they had been unable to procure their usual supply of drugs. Others who had not encountered this difficulty became aware of their dependence in other ways.

Most of the people I knew were all registered and we were all using and we used to meet down at Boots' corner and we would go in and get our scripts and come out and share it all out. But I never wanted to get registered 'cause I still had it at the back of my mind that I wasn't a junkie. That I didn't need it . . . Well I knew I was always into junk. I accepted the fact I was always into junk, but I had it in my head that it was because I wanted to be, know, and it was alright and everything was fine . . . When you start with junk, and you think you are using *it*, you are not conscious of the stage when it comes round and it is using *you*. You are just no' conscious of that happening . . . Anyway, the first time it sort of fluttered through my head it was when I couldn't get a vein anywhere in my arms and I had always said that I would never ever use my hands. And I had used my hands. And then I had always said I'll never use my feet. And I think the first time it really hit me what a state I was in, was that I had been sitting for about an hour trying to get a hit. It was terrible, there was blood everywhere. And my two feet were swelling up. I couldnae walk. I still didnae have this hit. And I was panicking cause the blood was all congealing—it would make you sick—here in the works. And I was straining the clots out of it and putting it in. And there was a lassie in the house and she was like that, 'Look just use your groin. You'll get a hit first time in your groin'. And it was the first time I used my groin and I was like that, 'Oh wait a minute'. That's when I first thought.   (Rose)

I didnae realise I had a drug problem until August when I asked them to get me into a rehab . . . the time August came and I was away down to five stone and I was physically ill. I mean I had hep and I couldnae keep any food down and I had a heavy shortage of veins. I was hitting up in my neck because I couldn't get veins anywhere else so everything was just collapsing and I says, 'Well I've got a drug problem'. Everybody I was seeing was saying, 'Look at the state of you, you look terrible'. My neck was all bruises, and all big lumps and all that were popping oot my neck, big scars and scabs over my hands and I was limping because my foot was done in and I was just a total wreck.   (Louise)

None of the women had set out with the intention of becoming addicted, and each was surprised when it became clear that she was:

I was just snorting it and then it was just like at the weekend—just a case of a Friday night and then it was a case of 'Oh it's Saturday night come on, let's snort' and then I only needed about a fiver's worth because the heroin was mair . . . better quality, and then it was, 'Och it's Sunday, it's a boring day', so that was another excuse to have it. And then one time I must have had it for about three weeks every day and I was strung oot . . . and I couldnae believe it had happened to me. (Michelle)

This surprise could partly be accounted for by ignorance. Some women believed that if other substances other than heroin were used, dependence would not occur. Helen's partner displayed this ignorance when he refused to believe she had only been taking dihydrocodeine (which in this instance was the case, as Helen had progressed to heroin). But others also believed this:

I didn't think I could get strung out because I was only taking difs. (Sandra)

You see I thought it would be easy to come off 'cause I had never experienced withdrawals or anything . . . and probably 'cause junkies are all related to heroin probably I would have felt a junkie from day one, but I never classed myself as a junkie. Alright I was injecting, aye, but I mean I never had any marks in my arms until aboot after a year or something of hitting. (Diane)

Another factor was that, despite knowing others who had experienced problems through their drug use, they did not believe in their own vulnerability.

You don't see problems because I mean . . . you know there can be problems, you know that you see poor souls, but that is never going to be you . . . That's just a blind spot. (Joanne)

My brother was a junkie for twelve years and, you know, I saw the state he was in and I says, 'No, it won't be me'. But indeed it was me. (Susan)

Being addicted had added one more reason to continue drug use—the avoidance of withdrawal symptoms. But it also had other repercussions:

At first it's great, you are in with everybody . . . but see once you get a habit it's murder. I mean, trying to keep the habit and trying to keep yourself respectable and all that, it's terrible. (Jenny)

The road from experimenting in order to be part of a crowd, for laughs, curiosity, to relieve distress, to feel good, had arrived at an unwelcome point:

I couldnae be like normal now, wake up and be able to get up and have breakfast and go out and do normal things. The first thing as soon as I woke up, it was my hit. (Helen)

I was going mental for money to get it. (Alice)

I didn't know what was happening to me. I just really started going doon and doon and doon and I just couldn't pull myself oot it. Just had to get money from somewhere to get a hit. (Diane)

3

Scoring and Grafting

Once the state of dependence is recognized and a decision to carry on with drug use is taken, two things become acutely apparent to the drug user: she has to make sure she has a steady supply of drugs to ward off withdrawal, and she has to find the means to do this. Until this point, drug use had been perceived as a *part* of her life. Drugs had been consumed as and when they became available, and this availability had not been recognized as an *essential* part of her life. This is not to say that purchasing drugs and financing this had not already become a major part of her everyday life. Becoming physically dependent requires that substances have to be taken on a regular basis over a period of time (Zinberg, 1984). But recognition of the stage of dependence brought with it a simultaneous recognition of the importance of the other features of a drug lifestyle. In particular, two activities assume major importance: obtaining a supply of drugs and finding the means, usually financial, to make this possible. The drug user's day becomes a typical round of using, 'grafting' for money, 'scoring' drugs, and using:

Wake up, have a hit, go away shoplifting, come back, sell all my stuff round the doors, buy all my kit, have a hit, maybe watch the telly and go to bed and the exact same the next day.   (Helen)

Studies of male drug users have found that to be a successful drug user, to maintain a habit, requires hard work, resourcefulness, and stamina (Agar, 1973; Fiddle, 1976; Finestone, 1957; Hanson *et al.*, 1985; Hughes *et al.*, 1971; Johnson *et al.*, 1985; Preble and Casey, 1969; Sutter, 1966). Whilst this picture of male drug users has become commonly accepted, the older view of male drug users as being weak and ineffectual individuals (Chein *et al.*, 1964; Cloward and Ohlin, 1960) tends to be applied to female drug users. Sutter (1966) and Fiddle (1976), for example, talk about the difficulty women have in maintaining their drug habit without a man to help them, and conclude that for this reason alone the drug career of the female tends to be short. More recent writings are divided over the ability of female users to maintain their own habit. Some hold to the old argument that women are maintained by a male partner (File, 1976; File *et al.*, 1974; Hser *et al.*, 1987; Prather, 1981; Smithberg and Westermeyer, 1985; Stewart, 1987), whilst others have found that women are more independent about providing for their own drug use than is commonly believed (Anglin and Hser, 1987; Kaufman, 1985). In the previous chapter, a woman's dependence on a man to introduce her to drugs has been shown to be only one way into that world. In this chapter we see that, even when introduced to drug use by a male, women do not need to rely on a man to maintain their habit. On the contrary, women are shown to be every bit as busy, every bit as involved in the business of maintaining their habit, as male users. They do the purchasing of their own and sometimes their partner's drugs, they finance their drug use themselves, and they run all the same risks, and more, from this lifestyle.

Purchasing Drugs ('Scoring')

We have already seen in the previous chapter that knowledge of where to purchase and from whom are essential requisites for successful drug use. Becoming known to dealers is also essential. The illicit nature of the purchases means that there is always an element of risk in the transaction, both to the buyer and the seller. Both have to be alert to make sure that the deal is not witnessed by police, and each has to trust the other. It is not unknown for police to pretend to be drug users in order to arrest a dealer.

However, becoming known and knowing from whom to purchase in the area in which the women lived was not too difficult:

You know people before you get into junk anyway.   (Susan)

They see you hanging about every day.   (Judy)

But becoming part of the network of drug distribution in the area does not immediately assure a steady supply. Illicit drugs are, like other commodities, prey to the vagaries of the market. Sometimes they are in plentiful supply, and at others there is a shortfall. There may be a shortage all round the city (the women hated Christmas, when there was always a shortage—drug dealers seemed to take this time to have a break from business; drug users, as Pearson (1987*a*) and Rosenbaum (1981) point out, never have a holiday). Alternatively, a local dealer may have gone out of business or been apprehended by the police. There may have been a general clamp-down by the police in the area, and dealers will have moved elsewhere to avoid arrest. Besides heroin being for sale, legally prescribed drugs such as buprenorphine or temazepam can be obtained from people in the community who are prescribed these drugs by their doctors and subsequently sell them either directly to drug users or to dealers (the interplay between drug users and the wider community and the subsequent effect on the local economy will be discussed later). If doctors become aware that this is happening, however, they may change their prescribing policy, thereby causing another type of shortage. All of these conditions affect the supply of drugs and contribute to the time taken to purchase. Scoring drugs, therefore, can take hours:

You spend all day. Let's say if you are waiting for drugs you can wait from nine o'clock in the morning till six o'clock at night.   (Judy)

Looking for drugs, sometimes that takes hours, up and down stairs, all round the area.   (Linda)

On one occasion I met Laura, Yvonne, and Judy in the snack-bar of the local community centre. The time was about 2 p.m., and Laura and Yvonne told me they had been trying to score some dihydrocodeine since 11.30 that morning. The day before they had waited all day until 6 p.m. before any became available, and even then Laura had only managed to purchase ten and Yvonne, five. They told me that the supply of dihydrocodeine was drying up, the reason being that some of the local doctors had become aware that their prescriptions were being abused. Whilst we sat in the centre Laura left every half hour or so, to go round to the shopping arcade which was just around the corner from the centre and where many of the drug purchases were made. Each time she came back disappointed. This went on until I left at about 5.30 p.m. The next day I met her again in the centre. She looked hot and flustered:

Avril you'll never guess what I've just been doing. I scored ten Difs there aff a guy that came into the centre and I was in the toilet trying to swallow them with some water when the next thing I dropped one doon the sink. It didnae go right doon—I could still see it. I've spent the last ten minutes trying to get it back up [*she showed me her reddened and scraped finger*], but it's nae use, I cannae get it and I'm strung oot and there's nae mair to be got oot there.

At times of shortages, being in the right place at the right time is important, but so also is one's status as a junkie. Judy explained:

There's usually people selling junk and that but if it's DFs and the like you need to wait for hours. You get some people that just walk along and get them 'cause they know them, but likes of . . . see if I went down there just after starting to take Difs again and I went down the arcade, I'd have to get back in with the crowd again to get them first.

Status may sometimes lessen the time taken to purchase drugs, but it does not necessarily lessen the risks inherent in such purchases. There are three forms of risk which the women run when scoring: being apprehended by the police, being 'ripped off' by dealers, and attack from other drug users. Some of these elements associated with drug purchases were apparent the first time Moira and Annette allowed me to accompany them on a shopping trip for drugs.

The street to which they took me was one of the main scoring areas. Purchasing drugs in the area was carried out in two main ways: in the street and from dealers' houses. The street area in which drugs were sold and purchased was in the main shopping area. This comprised an open shopping arcade, similar to those in towns all over the country, lined with shops on either side. At the top of this arcade was a metal barrier separating the pavement from the road. This was a popular gathering-place for unemployed men, passing the time of day by chatting to one another. Close to this barrier was a bookmaker's shop, another favourite gathering-place, with people hanging around its doorway. The remainder of the arcade was made up of a baker, butcher, greengrocer, small supermarket, chemist, and newsagent. At the bottom, the arcade was overshadowed by a block of concrete high-rise council flats, notorious in the area for the number of drug users and dealers who either lived in or frequented it. Opposite this block and round the corner from the arcade was a small sweet shop/café. This was a popular place with drug users for both socializing and purchasing drugs. At most times of the day this whole area was busy, housewives and mothers with babies and toddlers there to do their shopping and have a chat with others, the unemployed men hanging around and placing their bets. Just a few yards along from the top end of the arcade was the police station.

We met as arranged at 10 a.m. in the local drop-in drug centre, about half a mile away from the arcade. The centre was also used by alcoholics. Some of these were prescribed drugs such as temazepam to help them with their withdrawals. Some, however, sold them to the drug users. When I arrived such a transaction had already taken place, and Moira and Annette wanted to move on elsewhere.

We set off in my car, stopping at a little corner shop on the way to get some change for the intended purchases. In the car Annette counted the tablets she had just scored. She exclaimed 'Dirty bastard, he's only given me nineteen' (she had paid for twenty). But she laughed as she said it. Apparently this was a probable occurrence, and if one was stupid enough to let it happen then one had to live with the consequences or take revenge at a later date.

They directed me to a car park around the corner from the shopping arcade. We left the car and came out into the street at the police station. As we passed the station there were two policemen coming towards it and us. We walked on the few yards to the barrier at the top of the arcade.

At the top end of the arcade it was reputed that anything but heroin could be bought—temazepam, temgesics, DF118s, and anything else that was on offer. The other end was the heroin-purchasing area. In practice this divide was sporadic. Substances of all sorts were both bought and sold wherever a deal could be struck. We started out at the non-heroin end.

There were some men leaning against the barrier as usual. Moira approached them, asking, 'Any jellies about?' but they said there was nothing around at that moment. We walked further down the arcade and another couple of policemen passed us. Moira waited for a moment and then called over to a couple of young men, 'Any jellies around, any tems?' but they too said, 'No', and they joined us to walk further down because they too were looking to buy. The five of us continued our walk, Moira calling out across the arcade to various people, asking about the availability of drugs.

We reached the bottom of the arcade and there were more drug users gathered there. Moira spoke to a young man. He told us he had just swallowed two £10 bags because the police had been around and he was afraid he would have been searched and arrested. He tried to make himself vomit, putting his fingers down his throat. A very young-looking boy approached Moira and the two of them walked away. They went into the doorway of the sweet shop. The boy pulled out a dirty looking bag with dirty looking tablets in it: diazepam. Moira agreed to take them and then gave the boy his money, £4 for 10 diazepam. As we walked out of the shop, I asked her if she usually took diazepam. 'No, I've never tried it but as it's around, I'll see what it's like.'

We went back to the corner of the arcade and stood around for about twenty minutes. It was a very cold, damp day, and we were shivering by this time. Moira and Annette decided they would try their luck at a dealer's flat. We went back to the car and drove round the block. In the arcade Moira had done all the scoring, all the negotiating; Annette had remained in the background, apart from chatting to the people round about. But at this point she took over. The dealer was a friend of hers and knew her better than Moira. We went up almost to the top floor of a block of flats, but when we got out of the lift Moira said that she and I should stay where we were. 'She [the dealer] only likes one person at her door at a time. We'll let Annette go.' Annette went away, but was only gone a couple of minutes when she came back—'Nothing doing, there isn't any kit around.'

Back we went to the arcade and hung around again, but still there were no drugs to be purchased. So far we had spent about two hours with very little to show for our efforts. We then noticed that, along from the shop where Moira had scored her diazepam, there was a policeman and a youth. The boy was putting things back into his pockets. Moira explained that he must have been searched for drugs. She suggested that we should walk on to avoid the policeman's scrutiny.

We walked around the corner from the arcade and towards the local community centre and decided to buy a cup of tea in there, as much to warm ourselves as anything else. Outside we met up with some other drug users. We purchased our tea and went back outside to talk to the others. To shelter from the cold (the others were not allowed into the community centre because they were 'full' of drugs), we stood in the doorway and so could not see up and down the street. Two policemen suddenly appeared in front of us and each took hold of the youth at either end of our group. The rest of us scattered in different directions, leaving the boys with the policemen, thankful that it was not us who had been detained. Turning the corner towards the arcade we met up with one of the other boys who had been standing with us. There began a discussion of what was likely to happen to the two we had left behind. Would they simply be questioned or taken in to the police station for a strip search? We did not have long to wait to find out; just then the two policemen came round the corner with the two boys in custody.

We again walked down the arcade. Annette pondered what would have happened to them if they had been searched and their drugs had been found. Moira, however, had left nothing to chance on this occasion. She said in amazement, 'Have you still got the stuff on you? You'd have been charged with possession. You should have done what I've done—I've left mine in Avril's motor.'

Someone approached Moira and Annette and said that he knew of a score deal they could have. However they did not have the necessary £20. Just then, one of the boys who had been taken away by the police appeared again. He had been searched and had had nothing on him. He joined in the discussion about the score deal, and it was arranged that the four of them would pool their resources and buy the deal between them. Moira walked off with the boys, but Annette was cold and wanted to sit in the car. Five minutes later they reappeared in a Land Rover and shouted to us to follow them. We came to a stop outside Annette's house. She said, 'Well, come on then, come on, they're going up there to have a hit.' We went upstairs, the morning's shopping completed.

Going scoring is not simply a case of locating a dealer. It is a social occasion which provides an opportunity to find out where the deals are to be found and when. Drug users who know each other will share such information and sometimes drugs too. It is also an opportunity to discuss other matters of importance to each other, such as who had been 'ripped off' by whom.

Being 'ripped off' was a subject that was often discussed. The term referred to occasions when a dealer would either short-change a customer, by not giving the amount of tablets which had been paid for, or giving 'dummy smack' in which all, or almost all, the heroin had been replaced by another substance. The likelihood, if not certainty, that this would happen was regarded as part and parcel of the drug lifestyle, and discussed often with a philosophical shrug of the shoulders, or with a laugh:

It happened to Andrew yesterday—he got two empty bags for £40, I told him, 'That's what you get'.   (Kate)

Those new to the area (as Andrew was) or new to drug use were prime candidates for being short-changed:

You do get some people down here that do bump you, you know bump people from this area. But most of them, the people that bump down here, it's people from another area they bump . . . like they kid on they're selling kit. It is all wrapped up in cellophane so it takes a while to open it. By the time you have opened it they've gone away.   (Judy)

If you go into a different district you'd get ripped off.   (Maureen)

There's one wee lassie down here just now and she gets ripped off every day—*every day*. She's just sort of new on the scene down here. She's up the toon working from six at night till six in the morning and coming down here in the morning with maybe £200 and asks for £40 worth and they'll say they'll go and get it and they'll rip her off. So she's still got enough money left to give somebody else £40, and somebody else £40, and she's got to work hard to earn that and she expects to get ripped off three or four times before she gets what she wants, it's that bad.   (Kate).

It is in this situation, Kate argued, that one's status as a drug user can make a difference.

She's not like me, like not many people would rip me off because I'm well known. I've ripped guys off that I know could beat me up in two minutes but they don't because I've got a reputation . . . I've been a junkie longer than them and I've been on the scene longer, things like that.

Being ripped off is something that happens to all drug users, male and females alike. But women are more prone to another form of risk when scoring, that of being violently assaulted by other drug users who steal their money or newly acquired drugs.

I think lassies are more likely to get mugged and bumped than a guy . . . like that lassie that got mugged for the hundred and odd pounds that I was telling you about . . . if that was a guy I don't think those guys that did that would have done it to a guy. A guy can stand up for himself more than a lassie can.   (Judy)

Because of the illegal nature of their activities, drug users cannot resort to the usual legal channels for exacting justice, that of taking such complaints to the police. The acceptance of these happenings is bound up in the knowledge that the victims would either behave in the same way as the perpetrators in similar circumstances or that they will find some other way of exacting revenge. Kate summed this up when telling about the experience of Andrew, her partner.

If he sees the guy that did it to him, I suppose he'll probably do something about it, but he wouldn't go looking for him. You know I've done similar things to people. There's this big guy Jack, he was selling smack and I was up every day. It was £20 every day and the stuff was crap but it was easy to get, it was getting me by, every day £20 and then it went up to £30, £40, and this day all I had was a tenner, so I went to Marks and Spencer and knocked a pair of shoes and brought them back and says, 'Can I score for a tenner and these shoes?' But he wasn't in, it was the wife and she said, 'I can't do it, I can't, I can't'. So I said I would come back. Then she started pulling out a big package—about eighteen bags, tenner bags out of her pocket—and I just grabbed it out of her hand. I says, 'I'm just taking this'—desperation—'I'm just fuckin' taking this'. She started trying to fight with me, you know, and scratching my hand and all that. I wasn't fighting with her, just sort of pushed her away from me, I was just wanting to get out of the door, when who came in but her man. He says 'What's the score here then, what's happening?' I said, 'There's two guys with heavy blades, you'd better let me out or I'll call them in'. There weren't of course, I was just on my own. I had to think quick and if you have the brass neck to do it, say it, you'll get away with it you know.

In her study of female drug users, Rosenbaum (1981) argued that the risks attached to purchasing drugs formed part of the excitement that some of the women in her study were seeking. However, although the women in this present study were aware of the risks they ran, there was no sign that the women welcomed them or found them intrinsically exciting. Rather, they became a taken-for-granted aspect of their lives, and as such were not always at the forefront of their minds. The way their purchases were made also reduced the perception of risk. For some women, shopping for drugs became part and parcel of shopping for other items, and was bound up in the everyday organization of the community. Scoring was often carried out at the same time as buying groceries, nappies for the baby, or whatever, or broke up an afternoon sitting in the house or in the community centre. Many of the purchases were made either from 'respectable' members of the community who sold their prescriptions, or from friends, again lending an air of normality to the proceedings.

The effect of drug use itself could reduce the perception of risk. Explaining how one became known in a new area, Maureen told me:

When I went to Easterhouse I didnae know anybody, I just got an address saying this woman was selling. And I just went up and chanced it. I mean I could have gone to anybody's hoose, but I just took that chance. And true enough it was the woman. But I . . . you do really have to watch yourself. I think I was being too brass, but I was full of it at the time, so I didnae realise. I mean, see if I had had heroin or tems, I'd know what I'm doing. I won't do anything that I think I shouldn't do. But they downers I think they get you into more trouble. Because I was doing things that I wouldnae imagine doing . . . I mean it could have got you killed.

At times, however, circumstances made risks more obvious and likely. A women may be in hiding from the police or owe money to dealers. She may not want it generally known that she had either started to use drugs or had recommenced after a period of abstention:

I had been aff it and I met my old pal from school and she said she was selling it. And I went up to that lassie's hoose and I said to her that I didn't want anyone to know that I'm using 'cause it would just cause trouble for me with my Ma and Da. She knew that as well so she said that wasn't a problem. And I mean it was just like . . . it was safe to take, 'cause nobody knew. But after two months she stopped selling it and it was just driving me crazy. I was just left there. And I couldnae go to anyone else. I couldnae go down to the bottom of the flats and score aff anybody else. Then it'd've been all out in the open.   (Maureen)

It was possible sometimes in such circumstances to persuade others to score for you, but this was a costly exercise, as it usually entailed paying the purchaser back in the form of a 'hit'. I met Anne one afternoon in the arcade and she told me she had just been accosted by a girl who had been 'slabbering all over me and asking me to score for her and she'd give me a hit'.

Whilst scoring drugs in the sense of seeking out a dealer from whom to purchase was the most prevalent way of obtaining drugs, in times of difficulty other means of acquiring drugs were used. Some women, particularly if scoring had been unsuccessful on a particular day, would attempt to persuade a doctor to prescribe some substance, usually on the pretext of suffering from a non-existent painful condition, like backache or toothache. The success of this type of subterfuge depended on the experience of the doctor in recognising and dealing with drug dependence. Sometimes women were being prescribed drugs for their dependence and they would attempt to manipulate the doctor into increasing the prescription.

Fiona was receiving just such a prescription from her doctor, twenty dihydrocodeine per day. One night she had used up all her supply and could not afford to purchase any. She had called out the 'emergency service' doctor:

I didn't say I was a junkie—they don't come out if you say you're a junkie—you can't really blame them, they don't know if they're going to be mugged.

However, when the doctor arrived he was annoyed to find out that she was a drug user, and would only give her six tablets.

I cracked up. I said, '6 DFs are no good to me'. But he said he had to keep some for other patients. I couldn't persuade him. I told him where to put his DFs.

Other tactics were also employed:

Sometimes I used to . . . when I think about it! I used to go over to the doctor's and ask for cream for my spots and then fill in Diconal, you know forge them and then I'd fill in the back that it was for a pensioner, so I wouldn't have to pay for it. When you think about it it was really crazy. They chemists were giving me cream for acne for a pensioner that must have been dying of cancer or something to get Diconal!   (Rose)

Sandra allowed other drug users to use her house for drug taking purposes, receiving 'free' drugs in return. In addition to providing a similar service, Helen also injected drug users unable to do this themselves, again receiving drugs in return.

If a male partner was dealing drugs, such women could take their supply from them, either with or without their partner's knowledge:

I could always get a bit of kit, sneaking it, not that he would give me it. (Judy)

He used to get it all the time. And then I'd be down his house at night and it would be there for me.   (Jenny)

However, sustaining their drug use through non-financial means —using dealing partners' supplies, prescriptions from doctors, letting out their premises to users—formed only a small part of securing a supply. All the women at some time had to find the financial means to carry on using drugs. Being a junkie does not come cheap. Even those who either consider themselves or are regarded by others as having only a moderate habit need at least £20 per day, but usually much more:

At the moment I need about four score deals a day [£80].   (Kate)

Considering that the vast majority of the women were unemployed and relied on state benefits of, at most, £40–£50 per week, it is not difficult to see that extra money is required, nor to understand that, sooner or later, 'everything revolves around getting money to score' (Rose).

Supporting a Habit

There has been much written on the interplay between illicit drug use and other criminal activity (Anglin and Hser, 1987; Bean and Wilkinson, 1988; Bennett, 1990; Covington, 1985; 1988; Datesman, 1981; File, 1976; File *et al.*, 1974; Hammersley *et al.*, 1989; Hammersley, Forsyth, and Lavelle, 1990; Hammersley and Morrison, 1987; 1988; Hser *et al.*, 1987; Inciardi, 1980; James *et al.*, 1979; Silverman, 1982). It is sometimes argued or inferred that drug use drives users into crime, as if there is some pharmacological connection between the two.[1] Whilst it is true that the women in this study resorted to crime to maintain their drug habit, this was often the last resort when other methods had failed. Rather than being driven into crime, the women made pragmatic choices about how they set about raising finance.

Licit Revenue-Raising

A common response to the problem of insufficient financial means was to deprive themselves of other goods to keep enough for drugs:

Like when you get your broo money [Social Security] it's 'How much can you score?' And then maybe you'll blow it all and score as much as you can and you are left with maybe six quid odds and that is you to feed off that for a week. It doesn't matter, you eat or you don't eat . . . because you don't want to spend money on food . . . Once you have done it you don't feel the hunger, you don't feel hungry, but why waste money? I mean it is ridiculous. You'll no' spend money on essential things that you need. You'll stick shoes together with superglue, anything to keep your money together for scoring.   (Rose)

You spend all your money on drugs and you're starvin'.   (Lorraine)

---

[1] For discussion, see Hammersley *et al.* (1989).

When going without items such as food proves insufficient, selling items of clothing or household goods come next:

Everything I had I sold so I did.   (Sandra)

Like I was selling things out of my house, and all the stupid things that you could think of. I had a beautiful house, I had everything that anyone could want. I mean it took me to a stage where I lost everything . . . I selt everything out of the house.   (Jenny)

And then everything just fell apart. I had a nice wee hoose and a' that and three months later I had nothing in the hoose. Don't get me wrong—it wasn't a brilliant hoose but I had what I needed and I had my luxuries. Like I had my stereo that my Ma had given me for Christmas—that got selt —actually it got pawned and the pawn ticket got selt, then the tele went, then the video went, the washing machine went, it just all went doon and doon . . . 'cause that was the easy way just to punt things I had in my hoose because it wouldnae mean getting the jail because it was all my gear. Then that all ran oot so that's when I started shoplifting.   (Louise)

I'd never stole a thing in my life, never till I was right hooked on drugs and even then it started with me selling like decent clathes and decent jewellery. That all went before I could steal.   (Kate)

The evidence for these financial deals could be seen both inside the women's houses and outside. Houses were typically sparsely furnished, usually with a bed, a couple of chairs, cooking facilities, a television (drug users watch television a lot, particularly late in the evening when 'winding down' from the business of the day (Hanson *et al.*, 1985)). Usually there are no carpets, no luxury items, no pictures or ornaments, other than those which have little monetary value. Out in the street the women would point out a jacket or piece of jewellery which had once belonged to them but which now adorned a friend or neighbour who had benefited from their desperation for money.

None of the women liked living in such conditions, often apologizing for 'the state of this place' when inviting me into their homes and thus challenging popular conceptions of drug users as having no conventional social standards:

I ended up living in a junkie's squat. I've never been like that. I mean I've always been kind of well looked after, clean, everything, had everything . . . It was just a bed on the floor . . . lying about the floor on a bed. I'd never been like that and my Ma came into this house and my Ma was mortified. 'Imagine living in this, you weren't brought up to live in a den like this.' (Jenny)

Raising money by selling goods was, however, a limited option. There came a time when they had nothing left to sell, and some other money-making scheme had to be found.

Some women turned to money-lenders at this stage but found that this had inbuilt hazards:

I was right bad with money-lenders. They were charging like sometimes £7.50 for a tenner. I ended up owing them two hundred and odd pounds. I ended up they were meeting me at the Post Office and my Giro was going into my ain hand first and then straight into theirs.   (Emma)

For others, shoplifting and other forms of theft were the next resort.

Shoplifting, Theft, and Fraud

When all my stuff ran oot that's when I started shoplifting. But at that time I was only using tems, so to get kit, that was a luxury that was. I was getting that on my Giro day because I had money. I wasn't bothering about messages, so I had £42 to do what I wanted with and it was usually two score deals and twenty fags. That was usually what the Giro went on and then a score deal wasn't enough, so I *had* to go shoplifting. I had to get enough money to keep me going, so I started dae'in that.   (Louise)

Drug users are commonly perceived as leading chaotic lives. In practice, however, their lives are far from chaotic, but require to be carefully planned and structured if their goals are to be achieved. Shoplifting, for example, was often carefully planned, both methodologically and in terms of choosing items that would be easily resold:

In the morning I'd choose the clothes I was going to wear and iron them before going out shoplifting, so that I'd look alright.   (Liz)

I always go to weans' shops because you can always get weans' stuff selt. And they are wee clothes and they are easy to get. It's just a case of rolling them up and you are off.   (Jenny)

Shoplifting, however, could quickly become a career of fast-diminishing returns. In a city like Glasgow, with a compact city centre, unless very lucky or very successful, most shoplifters become known to store detectives and subsequently to the police, particularly if shoplifting is undertaken on a daily basis.

It got that I couldnae go into Glasgow because they knew me all over, so I started having to go to places like East Kilbride, Paisley, Wishaw for shoplifting.   (Helen)

I went to all different shops but they get used to you walking in and out . . . I only went elsewhere if I was getting a run through because I never had money for fares. I've been through in Clydebank a couple of times with a couple of guys that have a motor. But it's maistly always Glesga and as I say if you're going in and out every day your face gets known and it gets harder and harder. Likes of with Kate. Kate's known in every shop in Glesga, I think, so it must be dead hard for her to get a turn.   (Louise)

Whilst satellite towns can be exploited for a time the same pattern emerges. In addition, drug users cannot afford, in terms of both money and time, to travel too far from their usual scoring area. A bagful of goods or a pocketful of money are useless until they can be realised in drugs. Technical innovations, too, such as security tags on goods, makes shoplifting more difficult. For these reasons other ways of financing their drugs have to be found.

The women tended to use a variety of methods interchangeably.[2] Some revenue-raising activities were opportunistic. Drug users are constantly on the lookout for ways to obtain money, and through this vigilance an acute sense of awareness of opportunities for money making becomes developed. This was made evident on the day that Kate and I attended a conference on drug use which was addressed by the Lord Provost wearing her chain of office. While I was intent on her speech, Kate whispered to me with a grin: 'I wonder how much I could get for that chain in the pawn?' Women seized every opportunity to raise finance. They stole from family members:

My Ma had got a lot of Christmas presents and I took them all—she didn't even have them in the door and I had taken them all and selt them. (Frances)

I stole off everybody and the family put me out and my aunties took me in and I stole off them and they put me out.   (Sharon)

I stole my sister's dishes that she got for a wedding present.   (Sandra)

They stole from other drug users:

I stole one of the lassie's Monday book [income support payment book]. (Michelle)

Sally knocked £700 off another lassie.   (Emma)

---

[2] For similar findings, see Anglin and Hser (1987), Datesman (1981), Faupel (1987), File (1976), Inciardi (1980), Silverman (1982).

They stole from treatment centres:

I bolted from the rehab last night . . . I tanned the phone box—one of the residents helped me when I said I wanted to leave—we had to use a cushion to stop the noise.   (Kate)

They stole from anywhere and anyone they could. Handbags or jackets left lying carelessly around were easy targets, and could prove lucrative if found to contain cheque-books and cards. If someone was fortunate enough to come into possession of a cheque-book and card, goods and money could quickly be raised before the fraud was detected. This type of fraud was not always undertaken by the person who had stolen the cheque-book. Selling cheque-books was also a way to raise quick money:

You pay £3 a page, £60 if you get a full book. But if you had a full book you could make a lot of money if you dae it within three days . . . you don't buy it unless you get the card as well.   (Kate)

In my naïvety I wondered if forging somebody's signature were not a very risky undertaking. Kate's painstaking explanation revealed the necessary skills and knowledge required to carry this off:

It's *my* signature that's on it. You just use brake fluid, a particular kind. You just put it in a wee saucer with some Domestos, put the card in it and see the ink rising. It just takes their name aff and you just write, say, 'Avril Taylor' in my writing so when I sign the cheque it matches the name on the cheque and the signature on the card . . . You have to batter it all within three days before the notice goes round the shops. But you could go into the post office and cash cheques for £50 every morning for three days and if you had the brass neck you could go into their bank if you thought the person wasnae known. Me and Sheila just travelled round the city doing Marks and Spencer so that you could take the thing back and get the full amount for it. Buy a suit at £49.95 you get £49.95 back the next day, refund. Getting the full money instead of selling it for a third of the price.

The single end for which these various means were employed was procuring drugs. One occupation which could virtually guarantee a steady supply, without the frustration of going 'grafting' and having to then find a dealer to score from, was to move into dealing drugs oneself.

Dealing

Studies of drug users have acknowledged that women are involved in the supply of drugs, and that this constitutes a major role in supporting a drug habit (Anglin and Hser, 1987; Chambers *et al.*, 1970; Datesman, 1981; Ellinwood *et al.*, 1966; File, 1976; File *et al.*, 1974; Inciardi, 1980; James *et al.*, 1979; Silverman, 1982; Waldorf, 1973). Some conclude that this is by and large spouse- or partner-related (Covington, 1985; File, 1976; File *et al.*, 1974; Rosenbaum, 1981; Waldorf, 1973). More recent research has reported that involvement in dealing seems to be the most common illegal method of supporting drug use for women (Anglin and Hser, 1987). Women's role in dealing has also been portrayed as that of 'bag-follower' (File, 1976; Hughes *et al.*, 1971), that is, someone who forms a relationship with a male dealer as a way of procuring a supply of drugs. Whilst some of the women in this study began using heroin because of its availability through a male partner's dealing activities, none of the women had become involved with a partner specifically for the purpose of easy availability of drugs. Some did become involved in their own right as dealers.

There was a sharp distinction made between those who deal to sustain their own habit and those who deal for financial profit. Despite the necessity of both to drug users, the latter were reviled:

Likes of Mary Kelly. She sat in here one night and said, 'If it wasn't for all they junkie bastards' . . . no, 'if it wasn't for all they *daft* junkie bastards, my house wouldn't be like a palace'. 'Cause she selt . . . they buy their kit off her, their quarter ounces . . . 'All they stupid junkie bastards, my house is like a palace because of them' . . . If it wasn't for all them *buying* kit she wouldn't *have* a house like a palace. Somebody cracked up at her 'Aye my two brothers are stupid junkie bastards'. That shut her up. She boasts about her house and all that. She doesn't know what it's like, so people like that . . . I wish she was a junkie so she would know what it's like. (Judy)

Those who dealt to sustain their own habit were viewed much more sympathetically, but still excused rather than condoned:

Dealers that deal for themselves, you know pure junkies, need to deal to keep their craving going 'cause they need that much money. Like if they're hitting up smack and that and it costs a lot of money. So although they still shouldn't be doing it that way, that's just, that's it. But it annoys us, the ones that just do it for the luxury hooses and all the rest of it and they don't even touch the stuff.   (Alice)

People like me are just into punting kit to be able to get their hit every day. So you're doing it to really ... exist. 'Cause you'd dae anything for a hit when you're that bad.   (Susan)

Partly because of the ambivalent feelings surrounding dealing it is unusual for this to be the first foray into illicit money making. More importantly, it requires to be financed and requires a knowledge of the drug scene networks, neither of which is usually available to novice drug users.

Before one sets up in business as a dealer, drugs have to be purchased. Sometimes the proceeds of a 'job' are used for initial finance, as was the case with Judy's partner's dealing business: 'He got a turn and he got £4,000, so he bought kit'.

Like women in other walks of life, women drug users did not usually acquire such large sums of money through their work. Dealing for them had to be started at a much smaller level, or they could sell for someone else until self-employment became possible. Helen explained the mechanics:

We started going out shoplifting but my boyfriend got caught so he was a wee bit para' so I says to him that me and my pal could start selling it. We'd sell it from my hoose and cut it oot in my hoose. She'd put £20 and I'd put £20. At that time that would buy you a half-gram. It still does but the deals are oot of order. But at this time oot of a half-gram you could get six good, good tenner bags, so everybody would buy them, plus we would all get a good hit each plus maybe another tenner bag. We only had to make four bags really and the rest was ours but we used to make seven bags. I says to my pal, 'We'll make seven bags, that's £40 for oor next half-gram and a tenner each for you, me and Tommy and the three of us half the rest of the kit that's left. She said, 'But I'm putting £20 and you're putting £20. I told her, 'But we're dae'in it from my hoose, it's me that gets the jail, not you, so I'm no halving kit down the middle with you because if we dae that then I've got to give Tommy half my money and half my kit so you're getting twice as much kit as I'm getting and I'm going to get the jail for it ... no danger'. She said that was fair enough and that was the arrangement we made. So we started selling it and my pal's Ma found out she was taking drugs so she got kept in, so she stopped selling so I started selling for myself.

And then a half-gram wasn't enough for us so I got this guy and he laid a quarter of an ounce on me. That's £350 but instead of doing it all in half-grams and grams I made it all into tenner bags and fiver bags and that made me a lot mair money. And I made—I'll always remember this—I made £900 out of that quarter-ounce. See, if I had made that in half-grams and grams I would have made—you get seven grams to a quarter-ounce —so I would have made about—seven grams at £80—I would have made about £600. Plus my hits for the days that I had it so I would have gave him back his £350 and that would have left me with £250 but I made £900 'cause I was doing it in tenner bags . . . I can always remember this.

See the dressing table I have in my room, Avril? I used to have a big mirror on it and it slid aff. So I slid the mirror aff and put it doon on the bed and put the quarter ounce on it and see when it was chopped out it filled the whole mirror so it did. I made 90 tenner bags and we had tons of kit left, I cannae remember how much but at that time it was a lot to us and that was our hits. So I gave the guy, I don't want to say his name 'cause he's a heavy guy, I gave him the £350 back and that left me with about £550. That was mine and I felt, oh, this is good, great, so I bought another quarter ounce and that left me with £200. So I wasnae in debt because I had always said that I wouldnae dae kit for anybody, if I was gonnae get the jail it was going to be for me, no' for anybody else. So I paid him for the quarter ounce and bought another and cut it oot. We had good times, we had everything then.

It is easy to see the attraction that this lifestyle has for drug users (even if Helen's recollection of how many bags she had made seems somewhat exaggerated). If connections are good, a ready supply of heroin is available for personal consumption without the frustrations associated with finding money and scoring in the street. In addition, there is extra money available if the user does not allow her use to escalate (a danger which, as we will see, is real). Several of the women testified to the material wealth surrounding their dealing days:

I was dripping in jewellery . . . two rings on each finger and chains round my neck. Leather jackets, hundreds of clothes.   (Judy)

The wean never ever went without because I was selling all the time. I always had money and everything.   (Jenny)

For women like Helen, there is the obvious satisfaction of developing and using entrepreneurial skills,[3] skills unlikely to be fostered in the licit sphere. In addition, dealing brings with it power and status. In short, dealing for such women provides access to financial

---

[3] For similar findings, see Covington (1985), James *et al.* (1979); for further discussion of entrepreneurship, see Dorn and South (1990).

independence, material goods, and status which would be and was denied them in legitimate society.

Not everyone had Helen's flair for business, however, nor were other sellers as fortunate as she in having a supplier who asked for no more than a straight return on the initial 'loan':

They buy it and get their money back ... Like if you pay £1,200 and you get £2,800, that's like a profit of £1,600. So they get their £1,200 back right away. And then that £1,600, so like £800 would be theirs and £800 would be yours. Unless you get someone that's quite greedy then they'll only ... you'll get £500 or £400 or whatever and they'll keep the rest. And if you're stuck and you want to dae it, you'll dae it for them ... if you're stuck and you want money ...   (Susan)

For some, their role in dealing was merely a way to secure a supply of drugs and involved no cash transaction. Supplying drugs to others is a risky undertaking, carrying with it severe judicial penalties (Helen was 'busted' by the drug squad at the end of her first year in business but they failed to find sufficient evidence with which to charge her). Dealers at all levels attempt to minimize this risk as much as possible, and this creates a number of roles for those who handle drugs within the drug community itself. The closer one is to supplying drug users directly, the higher the risk of arrest. Dealers who deal in amounts such as ounces (who can be either drug users or not) will therefore sometimes persuade someone else (usually a drug user) to sell for them, and some financial deal will be struck between them.

At this stage, if the risk is still seen as too great another person may be recruited or subcontracted, either to sell the heroin or to 'carry' it for them to the point of sale. A female is useful in this latter role as, unless there is a female police officer on duty, police are less likely to pick up female suspects for strip searches. In this 'carrying' role, drug supply is often the only reward, the contractor having cut the heroin into the desired quantities, leaving no opportunity for further profiteering.

One aspect of dealing which can at first appear attractive, but can become a disadvantage, is that it makes 'getting stoned' possible:

Like when I was going oot and getting a tenner bag, it was just ... it didnae really look that much there, it ends up that all you get oot of it is getting straight but like if you are selling it then you can get enough to get stoned. (Susan)

Adulterated street heroin is of such poor quality and this, taken together with increasing tolerance as drug use continues, means that eventually 'getting straight' (a relief from withdrawal symptoms and a feeling of 'normality') is all that is achieved. But most users still hanker after the euphoric effects. Those who have access to large quantities can achieve this, although increasing tolerance means that they have to use more and more of their supply to sustain this effect. In this way a business can be injected away in a matter of weeks:

I bought an ounce . . . and I ended up I used it all myself. You know hitting up myself . . . I gave a lot away . . . I'd plenty of pals at the time, so I couldnae really charge them so I just gied them it. I got through it quite quick, within a couple of weeks.   (Susan)

Temptations such as this and the risk of arrest can make dealing a hazardous undertaking (Susan was awaiting trial for supplying, including supplying to a woman who had subsequently died from an overdose). For such reasons, dealing, too, was often used in conjunction with other forms of support at the same time, or alternated with other activities. If one plan failed, another quickly had to take its place. Usually the last resort for the women was to turn to prostitution.

Prostitution

The links between drug use and prostitution have been noted in many studies (Anglin and Hser, 1987; Cushman, 1972; Covington, 1985; Datesman and Inciardi, 1979; File, 1976; File *et al*., 1974; Goldstein, 1979; Inciardi *et al*., 1982; James, 1976; Marshall and Hendtlass, 1986; Millett, 1975; Plant, 1990; Van den Berg and Blom, 1985; Venema and Visser, 1990; Waldorf, 1973). There is disagreement, however, over the importance of prostitution in supporting drug use. Some suggest that prostitution is the most widely practised means of supporting a habit (Cushman, 1972). Others support the findings of this present study: that prostitution is not the most widely used means (Datesman, 1981; File, 1976; Hser *et al*., 1987; Inciardi *et al*., 1982). Only six of the women used prostitution as a means of supporting their drug use, two of them making this move during fieldwork. These women had all tried other means of supporting themselves,[4] and became involved only when these methods were no longer viable.[5]

---

[4] For similar findings, see Datesman and Inciardi (1979), Inciardi (1980).
[5] For similar findings, see Van den Berg and Blom (1985).

Prostitution was regarded by the women as a shameful occupation, and this was the main reason why it was seen as a last resort when all else had failed. In terms of an external cost–benefit analysis, prostitution provided a ready source of money with little risk of imprisonment (prostitution itself is not a crime, but soliciting or living off immoral earnings attracts a fiscal penalty). The fact of not being imprisoned if charged was a major attraction into prostitution for some women.

Well I'm out soliciting because I was shoplifting for about ten years and it got to the stage every time I got caught I was going to prison and I got to the stage where I was fed up with this prison carry-on, so the only way I can keep a habit going and keep myself going without going to prison . . . I mean every time I was getting the jail [convicted] I was *going* to the jail and I got fed up with it and I says the only way I'm going to get money without going to prison is if I go into the town and work.   (Lorraine)

I was fed up going to jail . . . I've been charged with prostitution but you only get a fine . . . about £100—you can make that in one good night on the streets.   (Joanne)

For some, the escalating cost of their drug habit was the spur into the lucrative area of prostitution:

It came to the stage that I couldn't shoplift any more to keep my habit going because I'd gone from tems to smack, so I couldn't just shoplift to keep my habit going. So I knew a couple of lassies that were workin' up the toon. So I went up the toon with them and found that it was easy to keep my habit.   (Louise)

Louise explained how she had taken this step and how financially beneficial she had found it:

One of the lassies had been up the toon and she had come up to my hoose to have a hit and she's sitting having a hit and I'm sitting rattlin'. And she said, 'There's a bag to square you up, there's no way I can see you getting money at this time at night unless you come up the town with me'. I went, 'Phew, I'm no dae'in that'. But I had to. I had to dae something because I couldn't sit strung oot all night knowing that I was going to be up all night and going to be ill. The two of us got a taxi up the toon. I got a skirt on and the heels and all that, didnae even put make-up on or nothing. I just went up and with me being a new face I think every other guy stopped at me, so I was saying, 'This is easy'. And the principle of it just didnae bother me after I made aboot £80 because I was saying, 'That's enough for the night, dae another couple and I've got a hit for the morning'. And it just—all my morals went right out the window, self-respect, the lot. I just didnae bother and then I started going up every night because it is easy money. You stand and you do eight punters and that's you got a hit and then you go back up and do another eight and you've got a hit for later on that night and one for the morning. So it's natural, it seems natural after a while. There is never a shortage of guys. There are always guys up there and you can do it seven days a week, it's no' as if there are any days you cannae go up. You can go up every night and even during the day you can do it if you've no' had a good enough hit in the morning. You can go to the Green [parkland in Glasgow] during the day and make mair. It's always there.

But, like some who dealt in drugs, and women prostitutes in other studies (Millett, 1975; Van den Berg and Blom, 1985; Wolfson and Murray, 1986), Louise found that prostitution could lead to a rapid escalation in drug use:

But it was just a trap because the more money I was making the more kit I was buying and the bigger habit I was getting. And it just—I got right in over my head—I just couldn't control it any more. I was making as much as I could and putting it up my arm as soon as I got it. Before I knew it I had a two-and-a-half-gram habit and I seemed to be up the toon every hour of the day, because I was having a hit in the morning and then going up the Green and making £40 and getting a half gram to dae me until I went up the toon at night and doing enough for a gram and hitting that and then went up for a hit later.

Despite Louise's earlier eulogy of the benefits of prostitution, part of the reason for her and others' increasing drug consumption was the nature of the job. Without exception the women disliked what they did and regarded it as morally reprehensible. Many of them also found what they did physically disgusting. Drugs were used as a mechanism to allow them to cope with the physical and emotional sides of their work, thus contributing to the increase in drug consumption (Goldstein, 1979; James, 1976; Millett, 1975; Van den Berg and Blom, 1985; Weisberg, 1985; Wolfson and Murray, 1986).

The first night I didnae go with anyone. I'd go up to cars and then say, 'Naw, it doesnae matter'. But the next night I got full of jellies. It didnae make me feel good, it just took the fear away.   (Michelle)

Lorraine and Sally told a similar story:

I mean *I* absolutely hate it. *She* hates it. I mean like some nights I'll stay with her and she'll say, 'You go out tonight and I'll go out tomorrow night'.

And the two of us are like *that* [*indicating their reluctance*] for about three hours before we can go out.   (Lorraine)

I say to Lorraine, 'Oh go home. It's just not you to do this, Lorraine, it's not *you* to do this'. She says to me, 'No, just *you* go home' . . . You really have to get full of it to go out . . .   (Sally)

. . . You know to get the courage to get up there and go because I mean . . . (Lorraine)

People think it's easy money, but it's not. I wouldn't do it if I had the money, oh my God no.   (Sally)

Louise, too, required chemical assistance to carry it out, in spite of her claim that it became 'natural' to prostitute:

Oh aye. There's been nights when I've been sitting in the hoose strung oot and to think of going up and doing the business just turned my stomach and I found myself in the toilet being sick because I just couldn't face it, you know, straight. So in they situations I would go and get tick because I couldn't go up the toon straight. I would have to be full of it to go and work. There was one time I did go up straight because I couldn't get tick from anywhere and I went up and the first punter I was sick over. I just couldn't do it. It was . . . my stomach was turning and everything and after that I always made sure I had a hit because I couldnae have gone up straight. Because you don't know the people and you don't know anything aboot them. Alright, they're using a Durex so you're no going to contact—get anything from them. But still doing it with somebody you don't—especially straight, when you're full of it you don't think about it, all you think about is the money, but straight, all that goes out your head. You could have wee weans, and you cannae face them. It's vulgar.

Drug use, however, was not always sufficient for everyone to over-come the dislike of work of this nature. Jean had moved into prosti-tution when I had known her for some months. She had found that shoplifting was becoming increasingly difficult because she was so well known. But her feeling of shame and disgust, despite her drug use, proved too strong to afford her much success in her latest venture. When she finally plucked up the courage to tell me what she was doing this became apparent:

I have wanted to tell you about it but I was dead embarrassed aboot it. I've been going on the Green and everything and see the Green, Avril, that's all old alkies. It's the old winos over the Green and you can only charge them like £2 and that.

During fieldwork 'working the Green' was seen as the province of only the most desperate, both because of the clientele, who were often alcoholics, and because of the low earning potential. Jean confined herself mainly to this area, as she did not want to be identified by other women working in the busier red light area in the town. In addition, to avoid sexual encounters with potential clients she would attempt to rob or defraud them, further restricting her success.

I don't do it all that often, just when I'm really desperate, scunners me so it does. Half the time you don't need to do it, you just, once you get the money in your hand you just run oot of the motor, you don't need to do the business. I've done that a lot and then because you've done it a couple of times they get to know you and nobody will stop you for business.

Amongst the women within the general drug using community, attitudes towards those who were prostitutes were divided. There were those who condemned it out of hand, regarding it as evidence of an intrinsic sexual deviance:

I don't know how they can do it. I think it must be something in some people. They just treat it like a nine-to-five job. Even when they stop drugs they go back to it . . . it's something in them.   (Anne)

Not once have I ever, *ever* thought of going up the toon. Not once. I think you already have to have that in you.   (Alice)

Others displayed a more sympathetic attitude:

I wouldn't say anything wrong about them, because it is easy money for them.   (Jenny)

Sympathy very much depended on circumstances. One rule in the drug community was that one drug user should never consider herself superior to another. There were good practical reasons for this rule. Nobody knew what desire for drugs would make them consider as a means to this end. Those who had not learned this lesson received no sympathy and no support. Part of Jean's shame was bound up in her knowledge that she at one time had condemned others for turning to prostitution. She therefore expected and indeed received, little comfort from her peers:

See to tell you the truth, Avril, we were glad when Jean started going up the toon. I know that is a terrible thing to say. I don't mean glad but . . . Jean was so high and mighty—she forgot herself so she did . . . She always criticized lassies for going up the toon, always. She hated them. It was like 'dirty cows this' and 'dirty cows that'.   (Helen)

The more sympathetic attitude of some drug users was therefore partly informed by the understanding that in the drug world one cannot afford to look down on others:

It's just something they have to do, for their hits, isn't it? I know I wouldn't do it. But everybody says that, don't they? But if you are that desperate you do anything.   (Judy)

Louise summed up the type of lifestyle that the desire for money for drugs leads the women into, and provides us with a hint as to why they continue with a way of life that many find unpalatable. Despite the dangers and risks involved in this way of living, and despite the damaging psychological effect of some of their activities, it is less daunting than facing a world without drugs:

It's just a vicious circle because you start using and it leads to shoplifting and stealing aff your family and tannin' hooses and working as a prostitute and getting the jail and getting oot of jail and starting using again and it's just always round and round until the only person that can break the system is you ... but that takes guts to dae that, because it's quite frightening being straight.

4

Social Networks

The previous chapter indicated that it is through social networks that information essential to obtaining drugs becomes available to the women. Rather than being simply instrumental in the pursuit of drugs, however, social networks and the relationships which characterize them serve other functions in the women's lives—functions which simultaneously tie the women more securely to the drug lifestyle. But whilst a drift away from 'straight' relationships is inevitable as more and more time is spent with other drug users, there is no complete severance from non-drug users in their community. Like Hanson *et al.*'s inner-city black heroin users (1985), the women inhabit two worlds, that associated with drug-taking and the 'straight' world. Being a drug user is one, albeit important, role played by the women. But they still continue to fulfil the roles of partner, daughter, neighbour and—not least importantly—mother. The next chapter focuses exclusively on the women as mothers. This chapter examines the significance of the other relationships in the women's lives, the impact that drug use has on those relationships, and the impact these have on drug use. We see how such interactions can help reinforce a commitment to a drug using lifestyle, and in the light of this we can begin to understand Louise's assertion at the end of the last chapter about the difficulties involved in being straight. What also becomes apparent is the falsity of the notion that women drug users are socially inadequate, isolated, or lacking in moral standards. An examination of their social relationships provides evidence to refute all these images.

Drug Use Networks

Junkie Pals

Extensive social networks amongst drug users are essential and inevitable, given the circumstances in which they lead their lives

(Hanson *et al.*, 1985). As we have seen, drug users supply each other with information about drug availability and the location of the best deals, and pool resources to purchase drugs. Given the uncertainty surrounding these relationships, however (acquaintances can be imprisoned, become abstinent from drugs, move into a rehabilitation centre), a wide network of associates is necessary to ensure a continuum of information. These relationships are not only developed within the community in which the women live but also fostered within establishments such as prisons and treatment centres. In this way, the very agencies set up to control and help drug users are also agents for the continuation of drug use. They provide the circumstances in which information can be exchanged and associations formed which allow the women alternative and more extensive sources of drug supplies.

I know nearly every junkie in Glasgow.   (Louise)

I've started going up to Parkhead to score, 'cause I met a couple from there when I was in a rehab.   (Maureen)

Sometimes such institutions were unwitting fosterers of drug use in more direct ways, with quite unexpected results:

I was in the jail and this lassie from Springburn was in and she had jellies in and she gave me a couple. She told me that she was getting a parcel on the Saturday—it was kit and jellies she was getting—and said she would give me some. And I was like that, 'Right! Yes!' So I was looking forward to this all week. But on the Saturday I was in the sitting room waiting for her when I heard my name getting called. It was one of the officers and she said, 'Your fine's been paid'. I went, 'Whit? No danger'. I was sick so I was. I was thinking, 'There's no way that daft idiot has paid my fine and me going to get a hit and now I'm going oot and I'll no' get one.' The woman couldnae believe it, she said, 'Are you no' happy to get oot?'   (Helen)

But Helen's fears at being left bereft of drugs were unfounded. Her friends outside proved to be just as generous:

As soon as I walked into the hoose I said to Stephen, 'Thanks very much you tit for paying me oot', and he said, 'Oh that's nice, isn't it?' And James was sitting there and Stephen said, 'It was James that paid you oot'. So I said, 'I'm sorry, James, I don't mean to be ungrateful', and I explained to him about the hit and he said, 'Oh well, maybe we can make up for it. Here.' And he's given me a score deal, so that was alright.

Sharing drugs with those who were strung out, whilst not a common occurrence (drugs were too expensive to be given away), did happen on occasion and is indicative of the understanding drug users have of each other's plight and their willingness to be supportive. Yet, when discussing the nature of their relationship with other drug users, the women emphasized only instrumental aspects, and denied that any bonds they formed could in any sense be called friendships:[1]

I don't have any friends, only my junkie pals.   (Judy)

Junkie pals were not regarded as friends because it was accepted that an essential element of friendship, trust, could never be part of such relationships:

You can never trust another junkie.   (Judy)

When they're full of it they're as nice as ninepence, they'll tell you anything, but see when they're not you cannae trust them.   (Laura)

Junkies . . . och they'd steal aff their best mate nae bother . . . if they were strung oot they would dae it nae bother. Best mate or no best mate. Everything can be all hunky-dory, brand new, but they'd dae it in a minute without any doubt.   (Alice)

They were resigned to the fact that stealing from and cheating each other was part of their lifestyle, and indeed there were many examples of this during fieldwork. Those dealing in drugs would short-change their clients and the same time run the risk of being robbed by them in turn. Kathleen had set herself up as dealer with money she had received from an insurance claim, but had been robbed of her stock by two drug using acquaintances, Cath and Dougie. Michelle stole another woman's 'Monday book' (social security payment book, so called because payments were cashed on a Monday). Anne had her television stolen by a woman drug user she had allowed to stay in her home. Acceptance of this type of action was based on the knowledge that any individual desperate for the means to score drugs would act similarly if given the opportunity. It was not passive acceptance, however. Cath and Dougie went home one evening to find their home and sparse furnishings had been vandalized. Michelle had to go into hiding for several weeks to avoid 'a doing' from the women she had robbed and her friends. Having exacted revenge, however, acquaintances could be

---

[1] For similar findings, see Parker *et al.* (1988), Stewart (1987), Stimson and Oppenheimer (1982).

and were renewed. Drug users need each other too much to allow malevolent feelings to flourish for long.

Yet in spite of this lack of trust it was obvious that bonds did develop between the women which were not only instrumental in uniting them against the straight world but which also challenge views of drug users as self-interested and uncaring.[2] Why the women did not recognize this facet of their relationships is more difficult to understand. Perhaps they had higher expectations of what constitutes friendship.[3] Perhaps the women's lack of recognition of the meaning of such behaviour was an example of what Mills (1940) has termed 'a vocabulary of motives' in which drug users themselves take on 'common-sense' understandings of their world—in this case, that drug users are selfish and uncaring and incapable of providing help and support to others. What was clear in practice, however, was that the women gave and derived support from other drug users at particular junctures in their lives.[4]

A common understanding amongst the women was that only other drug users could understand and sympathize with the problems associated with drug use:

Only junkies understand other junkies. Like see when you're trying to come off, people think all you've got to do is to make up your mind to it. They don't know what it's like to be sitting rattlin' and with your heid nippin'.   (Anne)

The women would help each other through withdrawal symptoms, advise each other over medical care, house each other when homeless, lend a shoulder to cry on through rough patches, and provide drugs on occasion:

We've been sitting up with Martin all weekend [through his withdrawals] . . . he's in a bad way. I think he needs medical help . . . I'm going to speak to the drug worker about him tomorrow.   (Kate)

Frances is going to try and come off tomorrow so I'm going up to sit with her and take care of the wean.   (Judy)

Karen's just had a big abscess which I telt her and telt her and telt her to go to the hospital aboot. I've had hundreds of them so I know what it's like. And I was like that to her [*indicating how serious she regarded the abscess*].

---

[2] For similar findings, see Faupel (1987), Gould *et al.* (1974), Rosenbaum (1981).
[3] See Rosenbaum (1981) for this view.
[4] For similar findings, see Tucker (1979).

But she's young, very young and I'm like that to her, 'You get up to that hospital. In the end I had to drag her to the nurse.   (Lorraine)

These really young lassies that are up the town and they don't realise the dangers of AIDS. And I'm like that to them, 'Let me see in your pockets. Have you got Durex? Don't do it without Durex, you can get AIDS.' (Sally)

Lynne's been staying here. She has naewhere to go and she's my pal and I wasnae wanting to let her roam the streets, so I've let her in.   (Laura)

My pal's wean was born with withdrawals and she said to me, 'See when I look at him and I see him all shakin', I feel so guilty, "Look what I've done to that wean".' I knew exactly how she was feelin'. I felt dead rotten for her so I did. I could understand everything that she was talking about. I just let her talk and greet it all oot.   (Helen)

Lynne was up in court and when she got oot she was strung oot and just wanted to go for a hit but her Da and her sister Margaret were with her. And Margaret says to her, 'Don't you dare come home with anything'. I says to Margaret, 'You'll need to get her some DFs and some jellies because she'll no' sleep and you have two weans and she'll have the two of them up all night. She'll be moanin' and groanin'.' But she didnae understand and said, 'She's getting nothing'. So I said to Lynne, 'There's my keys. There's 10 DFs in ma hoose, just go up and take them. I'll try and get myself some later. You've lain in jail all weekend without anything. I've at least had something. Just tell Margaret you're going to borrow some clothes and make-up.' So she took the keys and took the DFs, swallowed them and ran back up to Margaret's as if she never had anything.   (Laura)

The women developed a sense of identity with other drug users not only through reciprocal acts but also through their discussions related to their drug use and accompanying lifestyle. The illegal nature of this lifestyle meant that much of their activities, pleasures and concerns had to remain hidden from the larger law-abiding community. This not only resulted in an argot evolving amongst them but also meant that only amongst themselves could topics relating to drug use be discussed. It was only amongst their peers that that side of their lives could be frankly aired, and therefore only within this group that they could let down their guard and feel totally comfortable.[5] Such conversations did not revolve simply around the problematic areas of drug use. With each other they could discuss the successful aspects of their life and humorously talk about their failures:

[5] For similar findings, see Jeffries (1983).

Remember the time we knocked that huge box of cornflakes, thinking that it would be full of wee boxes we could sell? And then we opened it up and discovered that it was a catering box—just full to the brim with cornflakes. We ate nothing else for weeks.   (Sharon)

Aye. And I remember the time I took those downers and they made me feel as if I was invisible and I went into Littlewood's—I'd already been caught in there that week stealing·shoes and jumpers—and I went in and filled my bag full of knickers and I saw the store detective coming down the stair behind and these downers made me so stupid—I saw her and usually I would just have flung the bag and bolted but I was like that, 'She's just walking behind and she doesnae know I've got all this stuff in my bag'. And I went to walk oot the door and she just grabbed me and I got the jail. (Helen)

The sense of belonging to the drug culture was further strengthened by rules designed to protect the subcultural group from outsiders. The most important rule in this respect was that one should never be a 'grass'. To expose or denounce another drug user to straight society, particularly but not exclusively to law-enforcement agents, even to save oneself, was a serious misdemeanour. Joanne learned the repercussions of transgressing this rule the hard way. She had been operating as a carrier of drugs for a drug using dealer. One day she had been arrested by the police and signed a statement implicating the dealer, who was subsequently charged:

I was standing down between the café and the corner of the arcade. I saw two policemen standing under the high flats. Tony handed me the kit, five score deals. The two policemen walked towards the arcade. I walked towards the corner then walked back towards Tony. I stood a couple of minutes then saw the two policemen walking towards us. I threw the kit behind a pram and walked away towards the flats and then over to the café. Tony was with me at that time. When we reached the café the two policemen lifted me. They took me into the station and questioned me. They let me out about five or ten minutes later and then they went out looking for Tony.

No charges were brought against Joanne, worsening the seriousness of the offence in the eyes of the other drug users. Her behaviour was the topic of conversation for months, until Tony's trial took place. During this time she was ostracised and threatened:

Every time Tony saw me after that he'd say, 'I'm going to get 10 years for this'. He kept on saying, 'What did you throw it away for? Why didn't you put it in your mouth or go into the cafe and hide it?' He came up to my brother's and asked me to go to a lawyer and say that a guy frae Brigton came over and told me that unless I held the kit for him he would do in my boyfriend who is in the jail . . . I've had a lot of hassle frae the other junkies calling me a grass and saying I shouldn't be walking the streets and that I won't be for long.

Joanne found her position so difficult to cope with that she took drastic measures, including self-mutilation which would leave her scarred for life, before eventually seeking refuge in a rehabilitation centre:

I went on to heavy drinking through this to taking an overdose of pills and drink and I've slashed my arms three times. I wanted to die then but now I'm in this rehab and getting myself back on my feet. I've still got the court case to come up. I'm trying hard not to think about that at the moment. Tony says he's denying all knowledge of it.

At Tony's trial he was found guilty and sentenced to several years imprisonment. Joanne was not called as a witness, nor was her statement used. On the day the verdict was announced, however, despite Joanne's lack of involvement, feelings about her were running high:

Still, she was the one that first stuck him in . . . Anything than be called a grass. I wouldn't stick anybody in—she didn't need to . . . she'll need to go underground for a while 'cause she's going to get a right doin'.   (Anne)

But Joanne did not avoid her punishment:

Tony's pals, they gave her a doin'. Dirty grass. Nobody would sell her kit or anything.   (Judy)

It was several months before Joanne's credibility was restored, and even then this was the result more of her making her house available for drug use rather than of wholehearted acceptance by her peers.

Whilst this type of rule exerted external controls on group behaviour, the women also internalized feelings of group loyalty, which ultimately drew them closer to their drug using acquaintances and further away from straight society. One way this came about was through the women's awareness of the low esteem in which drug users were held by non-users in the community. Having once been a junkie, no matter how motivated she was to give up this lifestyle (discussed in a later chapter), a woman felt uncomfortable shunning her previous peer group:

When I came off and I'd only been away aboot a week and I went down the arcade and everybody's like that, 'Looking for kit? Looking for kit?' And I felt horrible having to say 'No' in case they thought that I thought I was better than them.   (Helen)

I didnae feel like talking to them, but I didnae want them to think I thought I was superior because I'm off it noo.   (Anne)

However, despite displays of group solidarity which served to separate drug-users from the straight world, there was also evidence of adherence to ethical and moral values associated with that world.[6] It was particularly evident in discussions about what the women regarded as unacceptable behaviour:

You get some of them that don't give a fuck. Some of them go out stealing wi' their weans . . . How can they dae that, Avril?   (Judy)

Aye and look at her down there, she takes her weans up the toon every night.   (Laura)

And she was pregnant. Up until a couple of days before she had the wean she was still going up the toon.   (Judy)

I mean some of these junkies down here, they're all walking about half boggin' and there's just nae need for it. Maybe like a week goes by and I've maybe no' done a washing but I make sure I've got enough clean clathes to do me till I get a few bob together to dae a washing.   (Laura)

As Faupel (1987) points out, however, and as we saw in the previous chapter's discussion of attitudes to prostitution, adherence to a stated set of principles depended on external constraints. Those whose drug lifestyles were operating smoothly could afford such principles. But at times the desire for drugs coupled with difficulty in obtaining them was often the spur to acting in ways they would otherwise regard as unscrupulous:

I used to say to people, people that didnae take it—like my pal Cathy—it was speed she was always into but one time I was strung out and I said to her, 'Cathy, kit's brilliant', and I talked her into wanting to get a bit if she had money. So she said, 'Want to come with me and try and sell my carpet? I was going to sell it anyway.' So we went away and she selt it and she got

---

[6] For similar findings, see Faupel (1987), Hanson *et al.* (1985), Preble and Casey (1969), Rosenbaum (1981).

£40. She says to me, 'How much is kit?' '£40' I said. But Avril we could have got a score deal but I was just being greedy. She said, 'But what am I gonnae dae, I'll need to keep money to buy a new carpet'. But I said, 'But Cathy, kit is brilliant', and I talked her into buying me kit. I gave her a hit and I was saying, 'See, it's brilliant, isn't it?' and she was being sick everywhere. And it was me that got Billy and Jack into drugs so it was. Getting them to go hauf with me one day 'cause I didnae have enough to buy myself. See noo, Avril, see when I look at the state of these two guys, I feel terrible so I dae.   (Helen)

In spite of the undoubted differences in behaviour that exist between drug users, however, the longer the women used drugs the more they identified with each other and the less they felt they had in common with straight friends.[7]

I've only been using about eighteen months. I've still got straight pals. It's no' as if I can't go back. But I've fallen away from them. It wasnae as if they pushed me away. I just couldnae talk to them.   (Vicky)

I don't know anybody straight. Nobody straight apart from my Ma and my sister. Don't get me wrong, I've got other people, like cousins and that that I could go to and they are straight. But you wouldn't go about with anybody or wouldn't go up to their houses because they are squareheads. Since starting drugs it's been, 'Oh no, no, this isn't for me being straight'. (Jenny, using for five years)

It was not only friendships with female non-users that became less common through a lack of mutual interests. Inundation of interpersonal relationships by drug users as drug use continued was also reflected in sexual relationships.

Male Partners

Truthfully, to go now with a straight guy, I wouldnae know what the hell to say to him.   (Helen)

Some women recalled having had boyfriends who were not drug users but found that they had to hide their drug use for fear of the boyfriend's disapproval or suffer the consequences:

Like if they don't take drugs they think *you* shouldnae. Like I know that when I was staying with Stewart and he'd found oot that I was taking junk, if he'd thought for one minute that I was taking it that would have been it

---

[7] For similar findings, see Jeffries (1983), Parker *et al.* (1988), Stewart (1987).

finished and the wean wouldnae have been here. I used to tell him that I was full of hash. If he had found out that it was junk that would have been it finished. Well he said that. He said, 'If I found out for one minute that you're taking anything it is finished'.   (Laura)

Some women attempted to abstain from drug use to meet the approval of a boyfriend:

I was going oot wi' a guy and he didnae like the idea of taking drugs so I came aff the drugs for ages, for aboot six month anyway. And then after a while I began getting into it again and that caused us to fall oot . . . It's just that when I've been going oot wi' somebody that doesnae agree wi' it I tried my hardest to come aff it.   (Joanne)

Relationships with non-drug users were typically undertaken at an early stage in the drug career. As the women became more involved with drugs, abstention to please a partner became more difficult and the women became exclusively involved in relationships with male drug users.[8] A minority of women were married; the rest had been cohabiting for periods ranging from one to eleven years. Promiscuity, in the sense of changing sexual partners frequently or having multiple partners, was not a feature of the women's lifestyle.[9] In this and some other aspects of their sexual relationships, the women held conservative and traditional attitudes.

Some women, however, were aware of inequalities within such relationships, whilst feeling powerless to change them. Their own more liberal attitudes were countered by the traditional sexism of the males in their community. Aware of this, some women had decided that steady relationships were not acceptable on such terms. Laura, for example, had decided that single parenthood was more acceptable than what she envisaged marriage or living with the child's father would be like:

He said that he would watch the wean and all that but I think that if I stayed up there and he wanted to go oot at the weekend and I wanted to go oot at the weekend and we didnae have a babysitter, he would be the one that would say, 'Well, you'll need to stay in and watch the wean. It's a woman's job to watch the wean.' Which isnae right and a lot of women have to put up with that. Having to stay in every night, day and night, every week-

---

[8] For similar findings, see Cohen *et al.* (1989), Eldred and Washington (1976), Kaufman (1985), Mondanaro (1989), Reed (1985), Rosenbaum (1981), Stewart (1987), Tucker (1979, 1982).

[9] For similar findings, see Tucker (1979, 1982).

end, while their men just go oot and do what they want to do. It's no equal, some of the men don't treat the wean as if it's theirs. I don't think so anyway. They think, 'Well you've had the wean' so it's the women's job to look after it or slave over a cooker. Which is a lot of crap because my sister's man, he looks after the wean while she goes oot to work. Cleans the hoose, goes the messages and everything. Some people think that that's poofy, but it's no'. That's just a good guy that you've got. You're just lucky to end up with a good guy like that.

For those women already in a relationship, drug use provided a focus of mutual interest, and partnerships were at times character-ised by joint support and effort in maintaining their drug habits,[10] each partner bringing to bear her and his own special talents:

We went out shoplifting together. Tommy was really crackin' at dae'in turns, but then he got caught, so that's when I said to him that I could start selling it . . . and I was keeping his habit as well. (Helen)

Me and Paul share everything. I mean absolutely everything we share. We have done for years. Paul's a good thief—it's nothing to be proud of—but it's the only thing he knows. I've always gone oot and done whatever I can. (Lorraine)

Aye, it's the lassies that dae most of the scoring and grafting. Don't get me wrong. See if the guy's good at dae'in turns and does a lot of good turns, then he can keep their habit. But see like if the lassies—mainly the lassies are good shoplifters, or lassies go up the town. (Jenny)

What used to annoy me was that I wasn't involved enough. I thought I'd be better at staying out of trouble than him . . . If it was something like a hold-up or that then I wasn't interested but if it was something like a cheque-book . . . I was always involved in cheque books . . . At first he didn't want me involved but then he had to admit that there were situations that it would be easier for a female to go into. So we had a sort of deal between us that I would do some things, like cheque-books, but he would always take the rap for anything that was found in the house. At first I wasn't sure about that, but came to see that it was a good idea. You see if the police kept finding only wee amounts around the house we were just going to say that he was an addict and I would help him to come off. Then if they ever caught us with a big amount I would say it was mine and that would be a first conviction for me and there would be less chance of me getting the jail. (Rose)

---

[10] For similar findings, see Farkas (1976), Kaufman (1985), Rosenbaum (1981), Tucker (1979, 1982).

Purchasing drugs, too, was carried out according to who was best suited in the circumstances:

I'm the one who knows where to score, Andrew doesn't.   (Kate)

When I was pregnant Stephen would go scoring for me because I absolutely hated going scoring then.   (Helen)

But where children were present more traditional roles often came into play:

We usually both go scoring unless it is at night and I couldn't go because I had to look after the kids.   (Donna)

Some male partners disapproved of the women's drug use if she became pregnant because they saw it as incompatible with the women's role as mothers:

I never told Donnie I was using . . . he would have cracked up if he'd known, he'd have given me a doin' . . . 'cause I was the one that has to look after the wean, so I shouldn't be using.   (Judy)

I was alright for money when he didnae know I was using. When he found out he wouldn't give me a penny, no' even for the wean.   (Linda)

He gave me a couple of bad beatings when I was pregnant because I was still using.   (Michelle)

He said I was a murderer because I was using when I was pregnant. (Angela)

My boyfriend didn't like me using, but he's a lot worse now that I'm pregnant.   (Liz)

Whilst concurring with the view that to use during pregnancy was wrong and in some cases was detrimental to parenting (this is discussed in depth in the next chapter), the women resented the fact that their partners expected them, and only them, to change their habits:

I think he's right to say that I shouldn't touch it now that I'm pregnant. But *he's* still using and if someone's shooting up in front of you it's hard. (Liz)

Aye he called me a murderer but *he* was the one that was encouraging me because he was still using and I was the one that did the scoring for both of us.   (Angela)

He was scared in case I wasn't looking after the wean right. But when I was using I didn't treat the wean any different. But he didn't help me. When he was using he didn't. Didn't feed her, change her or nothing.   (Judy)

Nevertheless the women did not question either the right of their partners to dictate their behaviour or the manner in which they conveyed such wishes—by using violence. Many of the women were subject to domestic violence, often so severe as to be life-threatening, but, like women in other walks of life, saw themselves as in some way to blame and therefore deserving of such behaviour (Dobash and Dobash, 1980):

Well, I was dead narky, dead cheeky to him.   (Judy)

He's given me a couple of bad doin's, but I couldnae really blame him 'cause he's taken a lot of stick from me.   (Sharon)

Whilst accepting this subordinate role in their relationship, what the women did resent—and what was a major factor in destroying a once trusting and supportive relationship—was the development by their partner of what has been termed the 'easy rider syndrome', in which the male partner lives off the earnings of the female (Wellisch *et al.*, 1970). When this type of exploitative relationship evolved, the women resented the burdens placed on them and came to see themselves as desired for what they could provide and not for themselves, seeing their partner's desire for drugs as having replaced concern for them and the risks that they ran:

I have to do the scoring while he lies in his bed.   (Anne)

I did the shoplifting while he lay in his bed.   (Linda)

Andrew only wants me for the junk. Who else would provide him with it? (Kate)

I didn't want to come out to work tonight but he's telt me I've no' to come back until I've made £40.   (Joanne)

That's how Robert started going out with Michelle. He knew she was up the town—'Och she'll keep me'—he doesn't hide it. He says it. But he doesn't have any time for her.   (Jenny)

A lot of guys stay with lassies that work up the town. It keeps their habits going. They don't really care. If they really feel for the lassie, then they will say something. But if they don't care about the lassie then, by all means send them up the town, it's easy money.   (Judy)

I had a phone call from him last night from the jail, asking me to go scoring some tems, put them in a balloon, visit him and put the balloon in my mouth and pass it to him when I kiss him! I don't believe this—he knows I'm just off it and I don't feel strong enough to handle drugs. And he told me last week that some visitor had been seized by the throat by prison officers to see if they had something in their mouth—and he wants me to do it! I'd get caught and end up in the jail and we'd lose the kids. Not only that, but he telt me he was aff drugs in there, he's just making a fool of me. He must be sharing works in there and he'll get AIDS. He'll come out full of AIDS. I hope he fuckin' dies from it. And he's always said I'm the weak one. He cares for nothing but his next hit.   (Anne)

Underlying Anne's concern about her husband's irresponsible behaviour was her own fear of contracting the HIV virus, this possibility arising from a facet of many (not only drug using) women's relationships: their relative powerlessness over the practice of safe sex (Richardson, 1987). Anne's immediate response to the news from her husband was that she would refuse to live with him when he was released. But when he was released, they resumed life together, an important pull for Anne being her desire to present a picture of a united happy family in order to retain custody of her children.

When an exploitative relationship superseded one in which the women had regarded themselves as equal, some women tried to assure themselves that their partners still cared for them. Referring to the fact that they supported their partners through prostitution, for example, they wanted to believe that it was only accepted by the men in their lives as a necessary evil:

We don't speak about it. It's not mentioned. It's just work and I've just said to him, 'Look it's either that or you see me in the jail so it's up to yourself what you want to do. You'll just need to accept it.' And he's like that, 'Just don't talk about it'.   (Lorraine)

Andrew really minds me doing this but he knows I've got to do it.   (Kate)

My man's in jail and I'm taking him up drugs. Now I've my own habit to keep plus his and he's writing me letters saying, 'You've got £61 a week and you're only bringing me up such and such'—like maybe two tems and some of my valium and temazepam I get off the doctor. And he's like that, 'What?' and I say, 'That's all I could do'. So I went up the town and did my prostitute. I mean I know my husband really loves me and see if he finds out, I'll lose everything I've ever wanted. I'm just a bag of nerves and I want to come off, and I haven't had anything today but I know that I'm going to go right down to that arcade and get myself a few temgesics.   (Sally)

The men's preference for the women's earnings, rather than concern for the toll such work took of the women, sooner or later became apparent:

He's just come back, at 7 p.m. without a thing—as if anybody stays out till 7 o'clock shoplifting. Now we've no money and he wants me to go out and make some. But I'm not going. I hate it. I can't be bothered getting changed and putting on makeup. He's not pleased, but I can't help it. (Kate)

Like at the end of the night maybe your man or your boyfriend sees you with £70 or something and they say, 'Och brilliant you can do that tomorrow night. But they don't realize how *mentally* that affects you. (Lorraine)

Relationships with partners, begun out of mutual interest, often became weakened when the drug needs of male partners began to supersede their concern for the woman. For the women, this stage heralded a period in which they unwillingly became responsible for the upkeep of both the domestic and economic aspects of the partnership. It has been argued that women in unsatisfactory relationships often have difficulty in leaving these because of economic dependence on male partners (Wilson, 1987). This, as we have seen, was not a factor for these women. The women were more than able to provide for their own needs. Yet most women remained in these unsatisfactory relationships. Sen (1984) has argued that people can also stay together for emotional as well as financial reasons. But, again, this did not seem to be the case with the women in this study, few of whom displayed any affection towards their partners or satisfaction with their lot. What seems a more likely explanation is that the women became too physically exhausted to be able to devote time and thought to changing their conditions. More importantly, their self-esteem was damaged by the realization that, in a culture in which there is an expectation of being loved and desired for oneself within a relationship, their role had become merely functional. Like the women in Mondanaro's study, 'not believing that they are capable of being loved, they settle for being needed' (1989: 18). Under such conditions, it is no wonder that drug use remained an attractive option, removing the stress of their everyday lives, lives which they eventually could not imagine being different:

You know, sometimes you meet some really nice guys. You know that they are nice, but just 'cause you're that used to a guy that treats you bad, you can't imagine having anything in common with them. (Vicky)

Families and Neighbours

The development of ties with other drug users did not result in complete isolation from 'straight' society. The women continued to interact with residents in the area and with their relatives, particularly parents. This continuing interaction arose to a great extent from the social structure in the community. The area consisted of multi-generation families who had lived in the area for as long as they could remember. Many people had grandparents, cousins, aunts, and uncles, as well as their immediate families, living in close proximity. The drug using women had either grown up with or been educated alongside each other. Where age gaps did not allow for this, older users would know the brothers and sisters of younger users, and vice versa.

I didn't know Anne was into junk. I've known her family for years.   (Kate)

Drug use was also so common that there were very few people who did not know a drug user, either because they had gone to school with them or because a son or daughter had done so. Drug use being so widespread in the area, non-drug users had developed a degree of acceptance that this was a way of life for many in their community. At the individual level, this could mean that sympathy was extended to drug users whom they perhaps had known since childhood. In particular, the families of drug users were regarded with pity, though not disdain—a constant fear of parents was that their child would succumb to the lures of the drug scene.

At the group level, local people displayed many of the common-sense understandings and prejudices associated with drug users. They distrusted them, often with good cause, many having friends or neighbours whose sons or daughters had stolen goods and money from their homes. They knew the heartache that drug use had caused in friends' and neighbours' homes, and felt anger towards the drug users for this. In particular, the threat of AIDS brought a new fear of drug users into their lives. In order to avoid detection from the police, who could use the possession of needles and syringes as evidence of drug use, some drug users discarded used injecting equipment wherever and whenever they were finished with them. This often meant that people would find them on the common stairs in the high-rise flats or in their back yards. With AIDS in mind, the locals feared for their own safety and that of their children. During fieldwork, a local drugs forum was set up consisting of local residents and professionals such as teachers, police, and drug workers. At these meetings, such fears were constantly raised.

Despite the undoubted disapproval and dislike of drug users as a group, drug using and non-drug using women could still congregate in the local community centre and talk to each other about the ordinary things that women find to talk about in all walks of life: their children, their schooling, the men in their lives, the cost of living, and so on. Contained within many of these conversations, however, were comments which confirmed the drug using women's different, and ultimately inferior, status in the eyes of others.

In conversations between drug and non-drug using women, non-drug users would invariably stereotype drug users' behaviour by use of the phrase 'you junkies'. But more directly derogatory beliefs were also expressed. One afternoon, a group of about three or four of us were sitting in the centre when we were joined by another young woman. One of the group, Fiona, had just had her children taken into care. Fiona was considered by other drug users as an exemplary mother, and there was considerable sympathy amongst the women for her plight. This topic arose again and the newcomer to the group, who had been chatting quite happily until that moment, turned to Fiona and said: 'Are you a junkie? I may as well tell you that I've no time for people like you. I don't think you should be allowed to keep your children.'

Drug users were considered not only unfit to keep their own children but unfit to be left with children at all. A common feature of life in the community centre was for women to perform babysitting roles for each other, allowing mothers time to go shopping on their own, visit DSS offices, or whatever. Judy, maintained on methadone and having forsaken the illicit aspects of the drug lifestyle, related how the stigma of being a junkie still stuck to her:

Janet wanted to leave her wean with Laura the other afternoon, but Laura couldnae dae it, so she said that I would be glad to. Janet doesnae know that Laura's a junkie and she said to her, 'No danger, I'm no' leaving my wean wi' a mad ragin' junkie. No danger.'

Waldorf has pointed out that the individual's concept of herself and subsequent role development depends on how significant others in the environment respond to her (1970: 379). All of us—and drug users are no different—want to spend time in the company of those who bring us some sort of reward, not with those who constantly confirm our inferiority (Ong, 1989). Social relations with the general community were, for the women, one more element in the identification with and gravitation towards their 'own kind'.

Interaction with the community also took place at an economic level. The women contributed to both the economy of the area, and in the process the community fostered the conditions for continued drug use. Other studies of illicit drug use have shown the links that unemployment and poverty have with heroin use. In particular, it has been argued that poor communities benefit from the proceeds of the criminal activities of drug users via the informal economy (Auld *et al.*, 1986; Johnson *et al.*, 1985; Parker *et al.*, 1988; Pearson, 1987*b*). In this particular area of Glasgow, where poverty was rife, members of the community were only too glad to buy stolen goods from drug users at prices up to two-thirds less than what they would have to pay for them in the shops. As Christmas approached, orders were placed for particular goods or sizes of goods. Not only stolen goods were purchased from drug users, but items out of their homes or clothes were also quickly snapped up when the women sold such items to purchase their drugs. Arguments sometimes developed as to who had first offered to buy a particularly sought-after item. In these ways the women users could be confident of funding their drug use through the needs of other community members.

Families

Like drug users in other studies, most of the women had parents who lived close by (Drug Indicators Project, 1989; Stanton, 1979; Tucker, 1979). The degree of closeness to parents was affected by the women's drug use, resulting in many cases in strained relationships.[11] Parents initially reacted to the knowledge that their daughter was a drug user in one of two ways, both having the consequence that their daughter would spend more time with, and therefore come to identify more with, her drug using companions. This is in no way meant to imply that any 'blame' attaches to family members

---

[11] For similar findings, see Binion (1982), Parker *et al.* (1988), Morrison and Plant (1990).

for the drug use of their daughter.[12] Other studies have testified to
the very real distress, confusion, and unnecessary guilt experienced
by parents faced with the knowledge that their child is a drug user
(Donoghoe *et al.*, 1987; Dorn *et al.*, 1987; Friedman *et al.*, 1988),
reactions which were not uncommon in the parents in this study:

If I hadnae been full of jellies I would never have telt my Ma and Da. To my
surprise it was my Da that took it worse. He started greetin' and everything.
I'd never seen my Da greetin'. And he's saying, 'This is all my fault'. You
know, blaming himself, and I was like that, 'It's no your fault Da', but he
said 'Aye it is, if I had done this or done that'. And I said, 'Da look it's no'
your fault, it's my ain fault'.   (Helen)

Another reaction of many parents was outright rejection of their
daughter:

My family just didn't want to know me when they found out I was using . . .
my Da didn't talk to me for a year. He's just starting to talk to me now.
(Judy)

When I started using my Ma threw me out.   (Louise)

I had nowhere to go—my family wouldn't take me in . . . my father wouldn't
let me over the door.   (Kate)

I wanted to talk to my Ma about it but she just didn't want to know.
(Angela)

Sometimes rejection was based on practical grounds:

I ended up living on the street . . . I ended up stealing aff of everybody and
the family put me oot . . . and I lived up closes and that . . . I had made
promises to all these people and they would try me again and I'd end up
doing it again.   (Sharon)

But another common reaction, whilst still abhorring the use of
drugs, was to provide support:

It's good to have your family around you, especially when you're a drug
addict. I mean you spend all your money on food and you're starving and
you can go to your Ma and Da and say, 'Ma, I'm starving and look at me I
need a bath, I'm boggin' '. I mean, I'm twenty-six and I still go to the door
and say, 'Ma, I'm starving, you'll need to get me a tin of rice'—you know
how junkies just eat rubbish—and she takes me in and feeds me . . . my kid

---

[12] A vast range of studies take the view that families are to blame for their child's
drug use. For further discussion, see e.g. Binion (1982), Kosten *et al.* (1984),
Stanton (1979).

never went hungry because I just took the wean to my Ma and Da and said, 'Oh I just cannae handle this any mair and he's starving and he's no' got a nappy, so you'll need to keep him', and my Ma says, 'Aye, nae problem'. (Lorraine)

My Ma used tae be feared in case anything happened to me when I was trying to get money for it. So she used to give me £7 to go for two tems and when I went to give her it back she'd say I'd just to keep it and then she'd start to feel guilty about giving me it.   (Donna)

My Ma had agreed to help me cut it doon. She would give me the money to let me cut doon.   (Helen)

Many of the women expressed regret at the effect their drug use had on their family, which in many cases the women considered was far-reaching:

My mother walked out one day and disappeared for six weeks. She had a nervous breakdown. I think it was the shock of finding my sister was also using. She felt she couldn't take any more. Anyway she came back but she's not living with my dad anymore—she was always supportive but he used to call us 'you junkie bastards' and she didn't like it. Anyway she's quite willing to see me and my sister as long as we're not using and that's fair enough. But I feel bad about what I've done to her.   (Liz)

My dad told me he sometimes lay in bed and plotted how to murder me. That's how bad I made him feel.   (Sharon)

There's three lassies in our family and there *was* a wee boy of twenty. And he died of an overdose and my mammy and daddy . . . if anything happened to me there would be three coffins going out not one. They just couldn't accept it anymore.   (Lorraine)

One night I was arguing with my Ma. She came to my bedroom door and I was having a hit and the room door was locked and Sheila, Diane, and Alison were in. And at this time it was really hard for me to get a hit. So she came to the door and I opened the door and said, 'Look I'm trying to get a hit. Why don't you get to fuck, they all hate you anyway, beat it.' Just because I was that strung oot and I couldnae get my hit. She took the weans and left my Da for three months. I was really sick after it. She put in for a divorce and arranged that my Da was to see the weans once a week. And my Da was greetin' and all that when they had to go hame. One day she came to collect the weans—she wouldnae come up to the hoose or anything—so I said I would go down and talk to her. So I went down and said, 'Ma listen please, gonnae come back?' She started greetin' but I never did it for me, I did it for my dad 'cause truthfully at this time I was too interested in my junk.   (Helen)

The degree to which the women were responsible for the break-up of parents' marriages is debatable, but there is no doubt that they blamed themselves, and that their drug use was often the catalyst for such happenings. Aware of and regretting the detrimental effect their behaviour had on their parent's lives, some women made the decision to stay away:

I just made up my mind I was just going to stay away from them, 'cause every time I was in touch it was tappin' this and tappin' that and really cheeky to my dad. And he just didn't need it you know, so I just stayed right away from my family—not that I wanted to but I felt it was the best thing for them.   (Rose)

I try not to bother my Ma with my problems, except when I'm skint and I'll tap her and not always pay it back. My sister's a hooker, that's how it's got her, and my mother's heart is broken with us. Aye, I can tell you what drugs is like.   (Frances)

The evidence presented in this chapter has suggested that through social networks, both in the drug world and in the non-drug community, the women come to identify more and more with their drug using companions. Rejection by wider society and a growing sense of alienation from it, together with the basic human need to be accepted and to feel a sense of belonging, all combine to encourage the women to become increasingly involved in the illicit drug culture.

The effect of drug use on one important relationship remains to be explored: that between the women and their children.

5

The Women and
Their Children

Much of the literature pertaining to women drug users has concentrated on the effect of drug use on the mothering role. In particular, the pregnant addict has been the focus of attention with the emphasis on the physiological consequences for the developing foetus and neonate (Carr, 1975; Caviston, 1987; Chasnoff, 1986*b*; Deren, 1986; Gomberg, 1986; Kroll, 1986; Women 2000, 1979). As Colten has observed, in many of these articles the mother is regarded as the 'independent variable' (1982: 78), as the source of the problem under investigation. With very few exceptions (Bauman, 1980; Bauman and Dougherty, 1983; Colten, 1982; Lief, 1985), scant attention has been paid to the attitudes and relationships which actually develop between drug using mothers and their children. Where this has been considered, those under investigation have invariably been mothers in treatment, and may not necessarily be representative of drug users in general (Bauman, 1980; Deren, 1986).

Feminists have argued that illicit drug use is abhorred in women precisely because it is regarded as a threat to the stability of the family, that women drug users are seen as rejecting the traditional role of motherhood (Ettore, 1985; News Release, 1979; Perry, 1979). With few exceptions (Bauman, 1980; Carr, 1975; Faires, 1976–7; Kaufman, 1985; Perry, 1987; Stewart, 1987), the drug using mother is generally regarded in negative terms. Some regard drug use by the mother as at least putting children at risk (Black *et al.*, 1987; Carr, 1975; Mondanaro, 1989; Wilson *et al.*, 1979), whilst others see it in stark terms of outright unfitness to be a mother (Densen-Gerber and Rohrs, 1973; Densen-Gerber *et al.*, 1972). These attitudes have been challenged in the literature (Colten, 1982; Hepburn, 1990; Lief, 1985), but their survival was highlighted recently in the case of a Berkshire baby removed from the care of its drug using parents because of the mother's continued drug use throughout her pregnancy and both parents' refusal to seek help for their drug 'problem' (Hogg, 1989; Levin, 1987; Perry, 1987; Walby, 1987). As we shall see, the women in this study considered that the majority of professionals with whom they came into contact held this opinion, that drug use *per se* was evidence of a lack of complete fitness for the task of parenting. Such opinions are, however, based on nothing more substantial than reliance on stereotypes of drug users, with little empirical evidence on which to base them.

So how does the female drug user relate to her children? How does she treat them? What are her attitudes to the role of mother? What effect has drug use on her ability to mother? This chapter considers such issues. It examines the women's feelings when pregnant and their expectations before and after the birth of their children. In opposition to the majority of the literature, which emphasises the effect of addicted mothers on children, this chapter also considers an often neglected aspect: the effect of children both as motivators for change in their mothers' lives and as variables in their mothers' continued drug use (Colten, 1982; Eldred *et al.*, 1974). Like Colten's findings (1982), it will show that drug using mothers' experiences of mothering and their attitudes towards their children reflect the attitudes of mothers in other sections of society. Drug using mothers expect to adopt the traditional caring role towards their children. Where the demands of their drug using careers make this difficult or impossible, like ordinary mothers with jobs and careers, they try to ensure that their children will be well cared for elsewhere, and, like other mothers, they feel guilty about abdicating from full-time mothering because of commitment to a career (Bernard, 1974). And, as in any random sector of society, there are those who do not provide adequately for their children (Bernard, 1974; Stewart, 1987). Such women are castigated by other drug users.

Pregnancy

It has been argued that in the female drug user there is a 'powerful drive' to become pregnant as a way of affirming her role as a woman, and as a way of achieving a close relationship in which she is needed (Densen-Gerber *et al.*, 1972: 786). Whilst some of the women came to see an established pregnancy as perhaps a way of helping them to change their lifestyle, none of the women had deliberately set out to become pregnant for these reasons. Indeed, most women's pregnancies were unplanned and, as is the case for many women (Kitzinger, 1978; Oakley, 1979), pregnancy sometimes came as an unwelcome surprise:

I was shattered, shattered.   (Kate)

I wasnae pleased when I found out I was pregnant but I'm dead against abortion, so I wouldnae get rid of it.   (Frances)

A common reason for not wanting a child was the woman's feeling that she could not cope, or did not want to cope, with the responsibility that motherhood would bring:

I didnae want to have the wean because I didnae think I could handle it. (Laura)

I don't really need the responsibility and the worry.   (Kate)

These feelings, common to many women, were compounded by the fear that drug use would pose additional problems. For this reason, two women had decided to terminate their unwanted pregnancies.

I just got a termination. I've already got a three-year-old and I've brought him up by myself. But it's not easy trying to cope with a drug problem and trying to cope with a baby.   (Vicky)

I didnae know what to dae. My Ma was shouting in my ear, 'Get rid of it, get rid of it', and my social worker was saying that it was my decision. But at that time I would have done anything to get back into my Ma's hoose and she didnae think I could handle a wean as well as a drug problem. So I eventually decided to get rid of the wean.   (Louise)

Another decided that she would give her baby up for adoption:

I'm no' keeping the wean. I definitely cannae keep the wean 'cause I've still got a drug problem myself . . . I know I'm not ready to look after a wean and drugs doesnae help it. I know I couldnae handle it the noo.   (Alice)

These women, however, did not take these decisions lightly or for selfish reasons. Rather, they felt that they could not give a child the attention that it would need; it was out of consideration for the child, and at considerable psychological cost to themselves, that they had decided on their particular courses of action. Vicky had recently had her pregnancy terminated, and was still wrestling with her ambivalent feelings:

It's no' what's best for me but what is best for the wean 'cause who knows what I'm going to be doing . . . It doesnae matter what you do, I think you would feel guilty anyway. If you bring the wean into the world and you don't know what you are going to be doing, and then if you give it away . . . The doctor says to me that I am worrying too much about it . . . I think it would have been a big mistake if I didnae terminate it. I had a wee boy when I was just seventeen. If it was the case that I was just against weans I would have had an abortion then. I went through with that one. I don't know. As I say it doesnae matter what you do, you are guilty anyway.   (Vicky)

Louise's termination had taken place almost a year before, but she too still suffered from feelings of guilt and ambivalence:

It's just like in October there when the wean would have been born . . . but see just about two hours before I went to the operating theatre I began to bleed and the doctor said that if I hadnae been in hospital I would have lost the wean anyway. That was the start of me having a miscarriage so if you look at it realistically I never had a termination. That's the realistic view but there is still that wee bit there. I suppose it's because the mothering instinct has been brought oot.   (Louise)

Alice acknowledged the difficulty she would have in relinquishing her baby, but had made her decision not only for the sake of her unborn baby but also to spare her own mother's feelings:

My Ma doesnae know I'm pregnant . . . she couldnae find that out. She's got enough worries . . . At least I'm giving the wean a life to live. When I go into have the wean you know I'm no' keeping the wean, but I dae want photos of it because I'm no' wanting to haud it after it's born 'cause it would only hurt me. I'm wanting to go in and out as quick as I can . . . Maybe if I wasnae on drugs at all it would have been a different story. Well I'd have been a different person obviously.   (Alice)

(Alice ended up keeping her baby. One of her sisters decided to tell their mother when Alice went into labour. The mother insisted that Alice should keep the baby. The last time I saw Alice she was still in hospital as part of the condition laid down by the social worker in charge of her case to show that Alice was a fit mother.)

For some, the knowledge that they were pregnant came too late for them to have an abortion.[1] One effect of opiate use can be amenorrhoea (Sonnex, 1987), and many women thought that they could not conceive (Deren, 1986; Kroll, 1986; Mondanaro, 1989;

[1] For similar findings, see Merrick (1985).

Rosenbaum, 1979; Sonnex, 1987). The absence of menstruation was not therefore taken as an indication of possible pregnancy; and other signs of pregnancy had to be present before a woman would begin to suspect she had conceived (Deren, 1986; Kroll, 1986; Rosenbaum, 1979; 1981; Sloan and Murphy, 1989):

I was going mental when I discovered I was pregnant. I was too late to do anything about it. I was six-and-a-half months pregnant before I went near a doctor or a clinic.   (Linda)

Again like other mothers, those who decided to continue with their pregnancies, once over their initial rejection of the thought of motherhood, began to look forward to the event (Oakley, 1979), not least because many saw it as an opportunity to begin a new life away from drugs.[2]

I didnae want it at first, but I love it to death already. I need something in my life. The responsibility will be good for me. I've never had anything worth while to look forward to or to make an effort for.   (Sharon)

I thought maybe it would calm me doon a bit—help me come off the drugs. (Laura)

It'll give me something to do, something to stay off for. Before this I felt my life was so bad I had nothing left to live for. But I think this will help me. I mean you can't go shoplifting when you have a baby.   (Liz)

There is a vast literature on the possible deleterious effects on the foetus from continued drug use during pregnancy, including low birth weight, congenital defects, early gestation, and neonatal withdrawal symptoms.[3] The exact mechanism of these complications is unclear, and it has been argued that other conditions, such as inadequate antenatal care, poverty and poor diet, and cigarette-smoking, could all be contributory factors.[4] Nevertheless, it is continued drug use which is usually regarded as the activity most dangerous to the foetus, both in most of the literature and by the

---

[2] For similar findings, see Deren (1986), Freedman *et al.* (1978), Griffiths and Pearson (1988), Hogg (1989), Kroll (1986), Rosenbaum (1981).

[3] For further discussion, see Chan *et al.* (1986), Chasnoff (1986*b*), Chisum (1986), Finnegan (1975, 1981), Fitzsimmons *et al.* (1986), Johnson Institute (1988), Keith *et al.* (1986), Klenka (1986), Kroll (1986), Mondanaro (1989), Stone *et al.* (1971), Zelson (1973).

[4] For discussion on poor obstetric care, see Finnegan (1981), Hepburn (1990). For discussion of the possible effects of smoking, see Fitzsimmons *et al.* (1986), Mondanaro (1989), Shapiro (1989), Stewart (1987).

women themselves. Most women were aware of the risks associated with continued drug use, and almost without exception they attempted to stop their drug taking out of fear of the harm they would do their child, and out of fear that the child, when born, would be removed from their care.

When I was pregnant I didnae take drugs all the time. I cut them right doon and then came aff them altogether. It was dead hard . . . I felt dead guilty because I was pregnant and I was dying for a wee lassie so I felt if I wanted this wee lassie that much then I could stay aff them and I did.   (Laura)

Well the last three months I was touching nothing. I was going to the hospital because of my drug history and I was feart of the social workers I saw there. They were taking urine samples but because I'd stopped it the samples were fine.   (Sharon)

I never took anything at all all the way through my pregnancy. When I fell pregnant I said, 'Oh taking drugs . . . it is terrible when you're pregnant.' (Jenny)

Jenny, however, was the exception, in that she managed to stop her drug using completely.

I found it easy to come off when I was pregnant because I hadn't used that much up until then.

Other women with more established drug habits, like those in other studies, found the attempt to abstain from drugs a constant battle which, when lost, caused them bouts of guilt (Burns, 1986; Fitzsimmons *et al.*, 1986; Rosenbaum, 1979).

Helen was three months pregnant when I first met her. The previous year she had had a miscarriage. Anxious that this second pregnancy should end with a healthy delivery, she tried several times to give up her drug use, with varying degrees of success. On one occasion she had been admitted to the maternity hospital to be detoxified. She managed to wean herself off the prescribed methadone and returned to her own home determined to use no more drugs. This determination lasted a week or so, after which she succumbed to temptation again. After the birth of her healthy child she discussed these attempts and how she had felt about her lapses. In the process she revealed that drug using pregnant women are as anxious and as fearful for the health of their babies as are ordinary mothers.

I never wanted a wean until I lost that first one. When I got my pregnancy test and I was told it was definitely positive I was dead, dead happy. The happiest I think I have ever been, but after a while I began to think that something was going to happen because of the last one. I said, 'That's it, I'm no' taking another hit'. I really thought I could dae it. And then people began to say to me, 'You cannae just stop having hits. It's bad for the wean'.[5] So I said to myself 'Yes! I don't have to stop taking it, I can just cut doon'. And I did cut it doon and then I started smoking it instead of hitting it and for me that was really good because I love needles, I know I do. I love having a hit and seeing the blood coming back when I pull it back and then pushing it in and the feeling. So that was really good for me to start smoking it.

At first I thought I would have a miscarriage. When I was kind of over that stage and I went to the hospital and they said to me, 'Do you want to hear the wean's heart?' I wanted to say 'No' in case they couldnae find it and then when they did I was dead happy. But I kept thinking the wean was going to be deid and see right up until I saw her, even when she was born she was a funny blue colour and I got a fright, even up until that moment I thought I was going to lose the wean. I'd heard of weans getting a fright when they are being born and they just die with a heart attack or something and I really . . . honest, if I was to fall pregnant again, I know I wouldnae use because I'd know it was a real wean. See to me it was a lump, no' a wean. It's hard to explain. I was scared to buy in for the wean in case it died. I only bought a couple of things just to show people I was buying things but I was so scared to buy things—no' because it would be a waste of money if the wean died—but because I would have to come home and see all the wee wean's stuff . . .

See when I was having her, sometimes when I was sitting and say I hadnae had a hit and I was strung oot, when I did try to come off it myself . . . you know I tried . . . I don't know how many times I did try to come off it myself . . . I would sit and I would say, 'I'm sorry wee lassie for what I'm dae'in . . . talking to my stomach. I only did it when I was by myself. I never done it when anybody else was there. But see before I was pregnant if I'd seen a woman talking to her stomach like that I would have said, 'She's aff her nut, she's mental' . . . But I think that was really luck that the wean was alright. I used the whole time so I did . . . I just used to take a hit maybe once a week or something and that was mostly—usually I make excuses for having a hit but see the heartburn I was getting, it was terrible and if I took a hit that was the only thing that took it away—but

[5] It is argued in some studies that sudden withdrawal can be harmful and can lead to spontaneous abortion; see Fitzsimmons *et al.* (1986), Mondanaro (1989), Stewart (1987). This argument has been challenged by Hepburn (1990).

with taking heroin, tems and things like that there must be some people can deform their weans or something and I kept really thinking about that. What if I've made the wean blind or deaf or something like that.

These fears expressed by Helen about the harm she might have caused her baby have also been found to be common amongst other drug users and other mothers.[6] The fear for her child's survival and her accompanying reluctance to provide for the child can perhaps also help explain previous findings that little preparation is made by drug users for their forthcoming child (Finnegan, 1981) and the difficulty they have in experiencing the reality of the child until it is born (Mondanaro, 1989).

The knowledge that she is pregnant also brings the drug using woman face to face with the possibility of one of the most serious repercussions of her illicit drug using lifestyle. She may have contracted the HIV virus and has the fear that her baby may be born infected (Henderson, 1990; Richardson, 1987). McKeganey (1990) has shown that the risk of passing infection to an unborn child is the most upsetting aspect of testing positive. Out of fear that this may happen, most women were anxious to be tested to see if they were HIV positive:

If I had had the virus I wouldnae have had the wean. And I'm against abortion but I would have. I think people with the virus should have the chance to have an abortion because it can make you go into full-blown AIDS plus a wean can be born and have the virus and then its blood can all change and it can be alright, but it can also always have it. If I had a wean and it had the virus I just couldnae bear it. I think I would be scared to love it, knowing that it was going to die.   (Alice)

When Kate was thirteen weeks' pregnant and waiting for the results of her HIV test, she spoke about her feelings:

She [the counsellor] said that even if I was positive I could still keep the wean. It might not be positive. But I don't think I could take that risk, do you know what I mean? She'd said that there was no need to hurry a decision to take the test but I said, 'I'm nearly four months pregnant. I need to hurry. It needs to be done this month because if I have the virus I would get rid of it' . . . I really would . . . I don't think they really know the odds . . . it means that you could be positive and the wean not but you

---

[6] For discussion of this fear amongst drug users, see Sloan and Murphy (1989); for other mothers, see Graham (1982).

wouldnae find out until the wean is eighteen months old. Imagine carrying a wean and then having it for eighteen months and you don't know if it's contracted the virus or not. I'd rather go through the mental anguish of having an abortion rather than the mental anguish of having HIV in my baby. I mean the two of them . . . one is as bad as the other but I could cope with an abortion. I couldnae worry constantly about a baby.   (Kate)

Sheila, who was HIV positive, found out what that anguish was like. One afternoon she asked me if I would take her into town for a pregnancy test. Sheila already had another child and had always said she would have liked a larger family. On the way to town she chatted about this, and how the other child would be thrilled at a new baby. She seemed happy and relaxed. The test was positive. Sheila said happily, 'I knew, I just knew I was pregnant'. She was laughing at this point and planning a trip to Mothercare to buy new clothes for herself and the baby. We arrived back at my car where, once inside, she promptly burst into tears:

Will the baby be alright? Oh, why did this have to happen to me? It could only happen to me . . . if I'd known earlier I'd have got an abortion. I can't bear to think I'll have a baby with the virus. I can't bear to think I'm going to die. What about Charlene? Who's going to look after her? What will I tell my mother and Donnie? They'll go daft because of the virus. Everybody will be saying, 'That's her pregnant and she's got the virus'.

Next day Sheila had another test carried out by her own doctor and to her relief it was negative; there was no pregnancy. But with relief came the realisation that, unless she could cope with the risks involved, her reproductive days were over:

I would love another baby. If it hadnae been for the virus I would have been alright but the thought of having a wean that's got the virus . . . you don't know whether it's going to live or die.   (Sheila)

The pregnant drug user, then, often has ambivalent feelings about her impending motherhood. Some of these feelings are those experienced by mothers in other situations. Others are more specifically grounded in the drug lifestyle. The women are anxious to produce a healthy baby, and guilt-ridden if they feel they are putting this at risk by continued drug use. Some see their pregnancy and the forthcoming birth as a chance to move out of the drug culture, whilst still fearful that this will not prove possible. Above all they want to be 'good' mothers and are afraid that they will fall short of their ideal or, worse, that they will not be given the chance to prove their capabilities.

Motherhood

Rossi (1973) has said that we know very little about what 'good' mothering is from the mother's own point of view. Similar to Dally's (1982) findings about 'ordinary' mothers, for the women in this study 'good' mothering meant always being available for their children.

I'm no' saying I want her to have all these material things and that. I want her to have more than that. I want her to have me all the time, any time she wants me.   (Frances)

I wouldn't dae anything that would put the wean at risk ... she comes before anything.   (Laura)

Papping her off to everybody else, I don't want that to happen. That's as bad as neglecting her.   (Helen)

When my wee lassie was born I was one that everywhere I went she came with me. See if I ever was walking doon the road without her everybody would shout, 'Where's Tracy?' That's how bad it was. That's how good I was.   (Vicky)

My Ma was never there and I get angry with her for not being there. I'm here for my wee lassie.   (Diane)

Many women, however, found that constantly caring for a small baby or toddler was stressful and tiring:

See when I had my kid I thought, 'This is gorgeous, look what I've got, isn't he beautiful?' With lovely wee pram, lovely wee suit, beautiful wee baby. I didnae think you'd end up with shit and teething and bokin' and greetin' through the night.   (Lorraine)

At first I didnae believe she was mine. You know you just keep watching her in that wee cradle thinking, 'My God, she's mine'. And I love her to death. But there are things I don't like. Early in the mornings I hate getting up. I've always hated getting up early in the mornings but I hate getting up to make bottles. And feeding. You've got to feed them at certain times and you've got to be in certain places at certain times to make sure she gets fed and change all these smelly nappies. That's another thing when you've got a habit and you're strung oot and you've got to change a smelly nappy. It's murder. That's one disadvantage that I just cannae handle. Apart from that it's brilliant.   (Laura)

My kid has got nowhere to play round about here. I'm at the window every five minutes. As long as I can see him I'm alright. I'm a bag of nerves. I never get a break from him.   (Sally)

Like countless other women who are prescribed drugs to help them cope with the stresses of domestic life,[7] often the women's response was a return to or escalation of their drug use, which assumed a different function in their lives at this point:

Since I've had the wean the thing that I feel maist is sometimes . . . some of the reasons why I take it is . . . I've got all these bottles to make up and I've got to do all her washing and I'm feeling kind of tired and then I'll think, 'I feel like a hit' and once I've had that I can go and do it all, dae the washing. It just gives me the energy.   (Helen)

I felt as if I could cope with her a lot better because I didnae know how to cope with a wean and I had them to relax me a bit and I felt I could handle it a lot better. I used to take them for the sake of being full of it and having a good laugh but now when I've no' got them I feel dead lazy as if I cannae dae my housework or cannae attend to the wean.   (Laura)

I couldnae cope with it and I think it was that postnatal depression that you get. I was living on my own with the wean and I just felt that everything was getting on top of me . . . he was needing fed all the time and changed all the time. I used to sit and think, 'I wish I didnae have him', but as soon as I had my hit I would be going, 'Come on darling'. And he could be screaming right in my lug and it wouldnae bother me. Whereas if I was strung oot he'd be doing my nut in.   (Michelle)

Apart from helping them cope with the physical and mental stresses of childcare, a return to drug use was also a way of helping them cope with guilt brought about by the gap between their expectations of having a baby and the reality of the experience. The women expected to find the task of mothering enjoyable, and as fulfilling all their needs, and were upset when this did not happen. As others have shown, this gap is also experienced by non drug using mothers, and can be regarded as a consequence of the 'myth of motherhood' into which women are socialized (Antonis, 1981; Badinter, 1981; Kitzinger, 1978; Oakley, 1974; 1979; 1980). In our society, the most fulfilling role for women is still regarded as that of motherhood (Rapoport, 1978). Those who are dissatisfied with this role are regarded as personally inadequate. As Oakley (1979) argues,

---

[7] See e.g. Brown and Harris (1978), Cooperstock and Lennard (1979), Ettore (1986, 1989*a*), Graham (1984), Stewart (1987).

only the most articulate and confident of women are able successfully to challenge this interpretation. Others less fortunate, including the women of this study, labour under feelings of inadequacy,
and hence of guilt.

Sometimes when I've taken a hit since the wean's been born I feel dead
guilty . . . Just guilty about having a hit when I've got her. I've got a good
boyfriend who is right good to me and a wean that's a crackin' wean
and you couldn't ask for anything better. I should be satisfied with that and
I'm no' . . . Maybe I've tidied up everything and I've changed the wean and
done all her washing, her bottles and all the rest and I think, 'I could go a
wee hit' sort of thing. But what about people that don't take hits and they've
got weans and maybe havenae got half of what I've got? Maybe their
boyfriend's left them and they've just got their wean and have no' got a
mother and father that will let them stay in their hoose so they're living by
theirself and finding it hard to cope. But they don't need drugs and they're
happy and that satisfies them and I've got a lot mair than them and I should
be happy and that should make me satisfied but it doesnae. It's still as if
something is missing. And when I take a hit that's the only time I feel really
as if I've got everything now. I dae feel as if I've got everything without a hit
but just the odd time I feel this life is pure boring. It's hard to explain but
people have got less than I have and they're quite happy and I've got everything that I want and I'm still no' happy, I'm still no' satisfied and that's
what makes me feel guilty. 'Cause I've telt you that I love the wean mair
than anybody else. I think that should be enough for me but it's no'.
There's still something missing. It's hard to explain but that's the reason I
feel guilty 'cause I've got everything and I just don't appreciate it. It's as if I
have got everything I ever wanted and I'm no' happy with it and I should be
happy with it.   (Helen)

Helen explicitly articulated the common feeling among the women
of this study that motherhood should indeed have fulfilled all her
desires. Implicit within this is the belief, a belief shared by non-
drug using mothers, that pleasures outwith this role are deviant
(Antonis, 1981; Ettore, 1989a; 1989b; Silver *et al.*, 1975; Wolfson
and Murray, 1986). Other women concurred in this view:

She's always been a sick wean, diarrhoea, sick, never eat anything. I feel
that I'm taking DFs and I feel I shouldnae be enjoying myself if she's no'
well.   (Laura)

I should've put my children first and stopped using. That's what a good
mother would have done.   (Fiona)

Returning to or continuing with drug use brings other dilemmas
to these mothers akin to those of other mothers who return to work

after the birth of a baby. The expectation that mothers should be the prominent, if not the sole, carer for young children is still strong in our society, and those who choose to put the care of their young into the hands of others in order to further a career are still regarded as less than good mothers. Many mothers thus feel guilty about depriving their children of the benefits of their undivided attention. The drug using mother, like others, is torn between her desire to be a good mother and the demands of her career. As we have seen in the previous chapter, most women, including those living with a male drug using partner, provide for their own drug habits and sometimes for that of their partner. Where the demands of their career did not interfere with child care, it was regarded as worthy of praise from others and as a source of individual pride:[8]

Fiona and Frances, fair enough they like their junk and they have their junk every day, but they have their weans with them twenty-four hours a day. Naebody watched their weans, neither of their Mas, you never heard them mentioning, 'My ma's got the wean'. They have the weans with them twenty-four hours a day, seven days a week. When they went to nursery they were there to collect them on time. And their weans arenae cheeky, they're great weans. Brilliant weans.   (Judy)

I know I take drugs but I don't get so full of it that I don't know how to handle myself or handle the wean. I don't take any downers or anything like that because I know that if I take any downers then I would maybe fall asleep and if you fall asleep anything could happen. Fire or anything. (Laura)

I don't think I'm any less of a good mother because I take a few hits because I still dae everything for the wean and she still comes first. On Monday there I only got £7.25 family allowance and everybody was standing around asking if we wanted any tems. Stephen wanted some but I told him he wasnae getting any. I said, 'The wean's got no nappies and she needs baby food'. And it was so hard for me to say no. Someone else said, 'Why are you no' wanting any tems?   Everybody says you've got £7.' I said, 'I've got the wean to buy for. That money is hers anyway and I'm no' letting the wean do without to have one tem.'   (Helen)

Most of the mothers in this study made attempts to balance the needs of baby and their career. In particular, they made strenuous efforts to keep their drug life from affecting their children:

I've got a drug habit but I wouldnae even consider going oot shoplifting. She comes before anything. If I was doon the arcade the noo and somebody

---

[8] For similar findings, see Rosenbaumn (1981).

came up to me and said, 'Do you want to buy a dress for the wean? I'll give you it for six quid', or if somebody said, 'Here's 15 DFs', I would take the dress. I've done it hundreds of times before. Done withoot DFs to buy her things.   (Laura)

I mean we can go hungry but no' way a child of three can.   (Lorraine)

In material terms, certainly, the women's children were well catered for, all of them beautifully and often expensively dressed and provided with plenty of toys. But most women were also anxious that other aspects of their lives should not affect their children:

I didnae want my kid to see people coming to my house and injecting. (Lorraine)

Like one day my pal came in to have a hit and she had the wean with her. I said to her to take her oot. She says, 'Why? She doesnae know what you are dae'in. And I said, 'I know, but that could stick in her mind—watching people having hits'. I didnae want her in the room.   (Helen)

They were all coming in, hitting up in my hoose. And he thought it was great: 'Just let them in, just let them in'. And I thought that was terrible . . . I had a wean crawling aboot and they wanted to inject in front of her and I would say no. I mean 'cause I didnae do it and I didnae expect anybody else to do it. But he thought it was, 'She is too wee to notice'. But it sticks in weans' heids at that age.   (Jenny)

Despite their efforts, however, most women had little confidence in their mothering skills.[9] Even when drug use was recognized as providing energy and tolerance, most still felt that their children were deprived in some way through their use of drugs. It was not, however, as Colten has argued (1982), that the women saw themselves as unfit mothers, rather that they thought they were not good enough mothers:

Like when I was using I didn't treat the wean any different. Oh aye, left her out on wee things like taking her here and there. In the summer taking her to the swimming and that. When you are using you don't do that . . . I wasn't neglecting her or nothing but she wasn't getting the things that she should get, like as I say in the summer going swimming.   (Judy)

They've not been hard done to. Maybe going places, maybe along those lines a wee bit. Because if I was strung out or straight I didn't go as many places as when I was on it.   (Donna)

[9] For similar findings, see Colten (1982).

My wean never went without because I always selt drugs and I always had money, she was always in the best of clothes. But she never got loved because you've got no feelings when you're on drugs ... I never used to cuddle her or anything like that ... 'cause see when my wee lassie used to go to my Ma's she would sit and cuddle my Ma and do all those things with my Ma. And then when I went and gave the wean to my Ma the wean was like that, 'No, I want my Mum, I want my Mum'. But she didnae really want her mum, she wanted to be loved. And my Ma could give her everything like that whereas I wasn't capable of giving her anything like that. (Jenny)

He'd never been neglected material-wise. He always had the best clothes and things like that. But that was the guilt complex, buying everything. If he ever wanted 10p it was, 'Here's a pound, here's two'. But I was never there for him, being away all day and saying, 'If I'm no' in when you come home from school go down to your Gran's'. My Ma was always there for us, always. She was never not there. It's wee things like that that my boy's missed out on ... when I look at him today he's no' turned out that bad. He is a good wee boy. I think he's dae'in surprisingly well with having me for a Ma. (Kate)

The lack of total confidence in their abilities did not, however, result in a universal agreement or feeling that women drug users were either incapable mothers or less competent than other mothers:

Some drug users keep their weans as well as anybody else. Some don't, just like some straight people don't. (Frances)

I don't feel I'm a bad mother. Like Sadie, she didnae take drugs or anything. But she's no' had her wean jagged [immunized] or nothing and the wean was right no' well and she never took it to the doctor. See the minute she's no' well I take her to the doctor's. I make sure I get her her jags and everything. (Helen)

Maintaining a drug habit and looking after a child do, however, present problems which some women find too difficult to overcome. Looking for drugs and finding money are time-consuming as we have seen, and without support many women find the effort of trying to keep separate motherhood and their drug career increasingly difficult:

Being a drug user and a mother—that's hard for some. (Judy)

See when Michelle had her wean, the wean was black. See when I saw Michelle just after the wean was born and you know how you look in the wean's pram and give it money. I went to give it a pound note one day and I lent over and see the smell that was off that wean! Imagine having a wean like that. If you ask me the wean is in the best place, with her foster parents. She's spotless now. And she never kept her access days and things like that. So how should she get her wean back? If she is really wanting to have him back she should keep her access.   (Jenny)

I mean the way Sally can say she's off to get money off that moneylender to go and buy drugs and no' buy anything to eat for that wean. I couldnae do that and I'm a mad ragin' junkie. I said, 'Sally, you cannae have that wean starving. Is this him going to be starving all this week again?' It's a nightmare. He's eating dried cornflakes. I mean pure poverty. Pure poverty. A wean getting up and eating bits of hard dried bread. Eating cornflakes with nae milk. There is not a thing else in the house to eat. She can live like that but a wean cannae. I've seen that wean going without food for two or three days. In fact I took him up to my Ma's last week. My Da took him and fed him. He said to her, 'I bet you've had a hit in the last two or three days'. She said, 'Aye, but I need it'. She's got herself in a really bad state. (Lorraine)

When circumstances such as those described by Lorraine and Jenny arise, some mothers find alternative care for their children. The majority of mothers in this study, like other drug using mothers (Chan *et al.*, 1986; Colten, 1982; Fiks, 1985; Silver *et al.*, 1975; Sloan and Murphy, 1989; Tucker, 1979, 1982), did look after their own children. Three had had their children taken into care. Five had their children cared for by family members, often the women's own mothers:[10]

My wee kid of seven, with me being into drugs so bad I decided that instead of dragging him aboot and seeing people injecting and me running aboot trying to get money and what have you, I thought that the best thing I could do was to give him to my big sister. She's got her own house and her own car and he's well settled there. She's had him since he was about three. I knew then that I was bad into drugs and I said to myself, 'Well I can't look after him, I'll give him to my sister, at least I know he is going to be fed every day'.   (Lorraine)

It's better for my kids to be with my mother 'cause even when I'm not using I'm in and out of hospital 'cause of my liver problems through drugs. (Emma)

I had eventually to give the wean to my Ma because I was like, 'Och I'm definitely going down hill and I know that'. Don't get me wrong, the wean

---

[10] For similar findings, see Colten (1982), Kaufman (1985), Lawson and Wilson (1980), Rosenbaum (1981), Tucker (1979, 1982).

never ever went without . . . But it was a case of getting up in the morning, taking them to school and all that was too much hassle . . . I mean like people coming to your door. I mean what is it like for my wean to grow up with that. I mean all the junkies coming to the door? I mean the wean used to whistle when she came up the stair and that, just like the junkies did 'cause that's what all the junkies do, give a wee whistle, and she'd say, 'Mum it's OK, it's me'. So I eventually went to my Ma and told her I was back on drugs, and she was like, 'Oh my God you are using drugs again, oh'. But I said, 'This time I've come to tell you to take the wean. I havenae waited for you to take her'. So my Ma got the wean.   (Jenny)

One of the repercussions of placing their child in the care of others was the reaction of the child towards its mother. Anne and Kate both had older children who lived with other family members. Both women suffered rejection by their children and both found this intolerable. Anne came into the community centre one after-noon, looking upset. She had just come back from a shopping trip with her daughter:

We had to cross Argyll Street and you know how busy it is so I put my hand on her shoulder to guide her across and she just shrugged it off. When we got to the other side she said to me, 'Do you mind walking in front of me? I'm embarrassed to be seen with you.' You know it hurts like a knife, like a knife going through you.   (Anne)

Kate's son lived with her mother. Almost all conversations with Kate contained at least one reference to her son, usually along the lines of how guilty she felt about him. She, too, was now suffering the same rejection faced by Anne:

I met him in the arcade yesterday. He just went to walk right by. He said, 'I don't want to speak to you. You're just down here to score.'   (Kate)

Whilst the existence of a social support network in the form of their families was obviously present for such women, such support was often offered for the sake of the children, and it was their interests that family members had at heart rather than those of the women.[11] Lorraine's sister, for example, had applied for and been granted custody of Lorraine's son, leaving Lorraine with limited access to her child:

[11] For similar findings, see Colten (1982), Tucker (1979, 1982).

My sister's got legal guardianship of him . . . I'm not even allowed to take him out. I'm not even allowed to take him out. I'm not even allowed to take him to the shops for sweeties.   (Lorraine)

Whilst giving her child to her sister had resulted in loss of legal custody for Lorraine, it was precisely to avoid having their children taken into care by the social work department that many mothers had opted originally to give up the care of their children to their families.

Social Work Involvement

Having children brings most drug using mothers into a relationship which they would rather avoid, that is, involvement with the social work department. Involvement with social workers was universally dreaded by all women with children;[12] yet few escaped such an involvement. Women would often come to the attention of the social work department during pregnancy when their addiction was revealed. As a result of this, most of the children still in the care of the mother were subject to some form of care order, in some cases a 'voluntary' arrangement between the mother and the department. Dread and fear were not occasioned by the knowledge that they were incapable of providing proper care for their children. We have seen that, in spite of having a poor assessment of their own capa-bilities, and falling short of their own ideals of what kind of mother they would like to be, most felt that their children were not totally neglected. Most were determined to try, and did try their best, to provide for their children. What the women feared, and had to face the consequences of, was that professionals such as social workers held negative images of drug users and had the power to take away their children on the basis of these images.[13] In particular, the women believed that social workers and other professionals with whom they came into contact through their role as mothers saw drug use as an automatic indicator of unfitness in a mother:

Our weans don't get treated any worse. Well some dae. You do see weans that are deprived but looking at my wee lassie you wouldnae think anything was wrong. There *isnae* anything wrong. But these social workers they don't go by the individual, they just grab all the junkie mothers, all the junkie mothers' weans. They don't take you as an individual. So you get lassies like me that look after oor weans but we're junkies and that's that. We've got a name tag. So our weans are no' looked after according to them. (Vicky)

I said to her, 'How can you sit there and tell me that people in an office could have a meeting and take my wean off me when they don't know the extent of what I'm using or what I'm going to be in the future?' (Kate)

Ironically, as we will see, the repercussion of the women holding such beliefs, which were not unfounded, was that the women developed attitudes and behaviours in response to their powerlessness which confirmed the negative views held not only by social workers but by people in general.

One universal belief was that social workers wanted to remove children from the care of drug using mothers:

We're the ones that get our weans taken off us. (Laura)

All they want is junkie women's weans aff them. (Diane)

I just do feel that social workers do take weans aff of junkies, don't give junkies a chance. That's how they come across to me—taking junkies' weans. (Jenny)

Even those who had been allowed to keep custody of their children felt that their social workers constantly watched for signs of failure in order to remove their children, and that therefore drug using parents, and mothers in particular, were under constant pressure to prove their capabilities in ways that other parents were not:[14]

It is just not enough for us to look after our children. We've got to be drug-free or we lose our kids. (Donna)

There was a television programme on one morning and it was about women with postnatal depression and my Da and my brother and me were watching it. And this woman told how she had this wean and it was a brilliant wean, never gret or nothing and one day he was greetin' a wee bit and she said she started slapping him and putting a pillow over his face and tried to smother him and the interviewer asked her, 'What do you mean, slapping him?' and she said, 'I just picked the wean up'. The wean was four weeks old, Avril, and she picked it up by the jumper and started doing that [*slapping*] right across the wean's face. And the interviewer said, 'Do you not have a social worker or anything?' But she said she had nothing like

---

[14] For similar findings, see Hogg (1989).

that. And Mark and my Da said at the same time, 'And they're giving social workers to the likes of you and look at people like that that are hurlin' their weans aboot'. You know even if it was postnatal depression, they are still dae'in it and they don't get social workers. I think it's all wrong so I dae and even my Da says that.   (Helen)

I know people that are neglecting their weans, but they don't get social workers. They don't have to prove themselves, no' even getting home supervision and then there is somebody like myself, probably hundreds like me and we're just getting rubbered.   (Michelle)

Moreover, the women believed that the images held of them by social workers were so strong that not only were they powerless to change such images, but no matter what they did, it would be interpreted as unacceptable behaviour:

It doesnae matter what I dae. If I'm no' smiling I'm no' copin', and if I am smilin' I'm no carin'. Do you know what they said at my last Panel?[15] That if I cried once mair they were going to put doon, no' that the wean was neglected or anything, just that her mother wasnae mentally stable to look after her. Because I was crying. They said that every panel I've been to I've been greetin'. I said, 'Aye that's right, you don't know what it's like. She's my wean. I came to you and said, 'Look, I want to help my wean. I don't want to put my wean through what I'm going through. I want your help and all you have done is to stab me in the back' . . . Right away they go like that, 'Oh a drug user'. There's a hypothetical question they ask me aboot straight away in a panel, 'What are you going to do if you have a hit in two years' time? That's what we're concerned about.' They shouldnae be concerned about two years' time, Avril. Do you know what you'll be doing in two years' time? Do they? They should be concerned aboot the time in the present and what's going on. They don't understand. They've nae—it's just that they think, 'Oh, a drug user'.   (Michelle)

This misinterpretation of behaviour was emphasised at an encounter between Michelle and her social worker at which I was present. We saw the social worker after we had visited Michelle's baby at her foster parents' home. Here Michelle had been told that at the baby's health check she had been found to be deaf in one ear, and that she would have to be re-examined in one month's time. Michelle was anxious when she heard this, and relayed her anxieties to the social worker when we met her:

[15] The panel of members of the children's hearings at which custody of children is decided.

What do you think could be wrong with her? The foster mother says she may just have a cold. Do you think that? Well, if she's still deaf in a month I'm no' leaving it there, I'm taking it further.   (Michelle)

To which the social worker replied:

Now Michelle, that's you regressing to your thirteen-year-old self again. There's no point in worrying for the next month. I feel like going out and buying you a dummy.

The attitudes of social workers towards their clients' mothering capabilities were also the more difficult to bear for some because they had asked for help, usually as a last resort, when they realised that their drug use was putting their children at some risk:[16]

Like me, I went to the health visitor. I know they are just as bad as the social workers. You think it will help you but . . . but they don't. The majority of the time they don't. I just told her so she could pull a few strings to get the wean into nursery so that I could get help with my drug problem. My Ma couldnae look after her all day if I went into a rehab. (Vicky)

They were therefore all the more resentful at what they saw as a total rejection of themselves and an emphasis on the welfare of their children.

But I was just stupid because everything was for the wean, the wean, the wean. She told my Ma that when I came back that if she sensed any drugs in me she'd phone the social services. But I mean that's what you're doing it for. You're doing it for yourself, but you are doing it for yourself to get better to help your weans. But that's the way it came across to me, every-thing was for the wean.   (Vicky)

Tellin' me that they're no' interested in me and this after I put her into care voluntary. Before that it was, 'We'll give you all the help we can', and then when I put her into care they told me that they couldnae care less if I had needles sticking oot of my arms seven days a week.   (Michelle)

Before they ever had my wean they would spend all the hours God sends with me—talk to me, but the minute they got that wean they just brushed me right aside. Which they've done the month since they've had the wean. I've no' seen my social worker since. Yesterday was my first access with the wean. It makes me say that they don't do their job right. All they want is women's weans aff them.   (Diane)

[16] For similar findings, see Griffiths and Pearson (1988).

If you've got kids then the help is not for you, it's for the kids. (Donna)

Once a child had been removed into care, most women believed that they would have little chance of regaining custody again. Rose had been drug-free for several years, but her view reflected that of those who were still using:

I know if I had a problem with junk again I'd be very wary of letting the social work department know about it because I'd be frightened that the weans would be taken off me. I think if my family were taken off me I would think that there would be no chance of me getting them back. (Rose)

When a child is taken into care, access times are given to the mother. The difficulties some women had in adhering to these access times were, they felt, unrecognized:

Sometimes I get so upset when I leave her with her foster parents that I can't face the thought of going there. (Michelle)

When she's been here to see me and she goes away she gets my Ma uptight for about three days 'cause she is upset. And that is very upsetting for me, so I sometimes tell my Ma no' to bring her. (Vicky)

Rigid adherence to access times was often used by the authorities as an indication of the mother's interest in her child or children and thereby her fitness to have the child returned to her care. Their lack of understanding of any difficulties this may have involved for the mother meant that any deviation from these times was interpreted as confirmation that the mother did not care, and was used as a way of limiting future access times. This practice, confirming the women's powerlessness, could set up a vicious circle in which women would behave in ways which confirmed the image of them as out of control and therefore unfit to look after children:

Monday, Wednesday, and Friday from twelve o'clock until three o'clock, that was all I had her and I never missed an access visit. One Wednesday my boyfriend had a huge abscess on his arm and he collapsed oot on the street and it kept me twenty minutes late for the access 'cause I took him to the hospital and the social worker said I loved my boyfriend more than the wean. I put him first. I said, 'What did you want me to do? Walk over him and leave him in the street? I panicked and I just rushed him to the hospital. I really did panic.' There was another social worker there as well as mine and he said, 'Oh well, you're too late for your access today and if you miss your access again you'll never see your wean again. You'll be lucky if you even see her when she's sixteen.' I could hear my wee lassie shouting in the back. I said, 'I'm no' leaving here until I see my wean'. He says, 'We'll just get the polis'. I says, 'Just you do that, but I'll tell you another thing, when the polis come they'll have to jail me and I'll give them something to jail me for'. I said to my social worker, 'I'm gonnae batter you'. She said, 'I don't have to stand here and take these threats'. I said, 'I don't have to take them from you either'. I said, 'My wean's shouting on me. What's wrong I just cannae go and see her. If I don't get my access today just let me see her'. They said, 'No you're too upset now to see her'. By this time I was greetin' and all that. So I said, 'Well fuck the lot of you I'll go and find her then'. So I started kicking in all the doors of the social work department . . . I just couldnae take any mair.   (Diane)

Believing, as we have seen, that social workers saw drug use as a reason either to remove children into care or at least to apply for a care order, one way in which women tried to avoid this was to lie about their current drug consumption. After the birth of her child, Helen had been allowed to take her baby home. Her strenuous efforts to reduce her drug intake, together with the fact that she lived with her mother and father, had reassured her social worker that Helen's baby would be adequately looked after. She had been asked, however, if she would be prepared to accept a 'voluntary' arrangement of social work involvement whereby a social worker would visit from time to time and Helen would provide urine samples as evidence of her drug-free state. She had agreed to this. One of her samples had shown positive and she had been confronted by the social worker. Helen had been careful not to use drugs for several days prior to giving a sample, and was convinced that either her sample had been mixed up with someone else's or someone had told the social worker that she was using again. Her social worker's accusation, she felt, was a test of her truthfulness and, implicitly, a test of her adequacy as a mother:

I had had a couple of hits since I've had the wean as you know and then that urine test came up positive. Now I don't know if they are just saying that or no', 'cause the last hit I had was a week before that . . . I only had about a £7 hit and it stayed in my system for a week? The doctor told me that it only stays in your system for three days—five at the very maist. And that's only if it's a big hit. So I don't know if they were saying that to catch me oot or if it did come up positive. But, anyway, as far as they were concerned I was still using. But I said to my social worker, 'No, I'm no' using it'. And I said it 'cause I don't need help the noo. I just feel like a hit noo and again and the wean is still brand new. The social worker herself said that to me. When she found out the sample was positive she said, 'I'm no' here to talk aboot anybody's weans 'cause the wean's brand new even if you are using. I see the wean is fine and every time I see you the wean is with you all the time and she's always well cared for, always spotlessly clean, everything is crackin'—her wee clothes and everything. And your Ma and that's there and the wean's getting all the love she needs. But it's you I'm worried about because if you are using I would like to help you.' But, Avril, I don't trust social workers. I don't care what anybody says. My social worker, she's the one that got Patricia's weans taken aff her for six months. Up until Patricia told me this I trusted my social worker. I would have said to her, 'Listen, I have had a few hits'. But since hearing that my trust has gone because Patricia said to me, 'She acts that nice and trusting towards you, but she's just trying to suss you oot'. A lot of people have told me that, Avril, that social workers are trying to suss you oot . . . my drug worker has said to me that because I volunteered to have a social worker I can get rid of her any time I want. But I didn't really volunteer. They said to me in hospital, 'Would you mind having a social worker?' and I said, 'No'. What would they have thought if I'd said, 'Yes?' What would they think now if I said I wanted rid of her?   (Helen)

Most drug using mothers, then, like other mothers, attempt to do the best for their children. The majority of children in this study who lived with their mothers were loved, taken pride in, and well cared for. The women saw motherhood as an important function, and when they sensed that their efforts to care for their children were being hampered by their use of drugs, most tried to ensure that the children were well cared for elsewhere. Nor was this apparent abdication from responsibility embarked on with any feeling of relief. Rather, the mothers adhered to the tradition that mothering should be their responsibility and totally fulfilling, and the realization that it was not was the cause of much guilt and anxiety, often accompanied by a return to or escalation of drug use.

But the role of mother also brings the women face to face with some of the negative attitudes held by others about them. To protect themselves from the repercussions of these attitudes, the women adopted defensive attitudes and behaviours. Whilst these behaviours are understandable, they confirm the negative images of them held by social workers and society in general—that they are liars and inherently deviant and therefore unfit to be mothers—and ultimately threaten their relationship with their children. Losing children can be the impetus for further drug taking and further integration into the drug lifestyle (Griffiths and Pearson, 1988; Matthews, 1990):

Look at Fiona. See since the weans got taken away, she's just gone doon and doon and doon. She's mad wi' it all the time and working up the toon noo to pay for her habit.   (Judy)

This loss can also act as a spur to coming off drugs, as we will see in the next chapter.

6

Coming Off

Sooner or later, all the women wanted to give up their use of drugs. This chapter will examine the reasons for this and the factors which made giving up difficult. It will be seen that, just as there are various reasons for beginning to use drugs, there are a myriad of reasons for wanting to cease drug taking,[1] for continuing or for beginning again.

Every woman made at least one attempt to stop her drug use during the period of my fieldwork. When I first met Michelle she had been 'off' drugs for three days; a few days later she had resumed use. Towards the end of fieldwork she entered a drug rehabilitation centre for a few weeks and then again resumed drug use. Kate had just come out of a hospital where she had been detoxified. Her abstention lasted one day. Through the fieldwork period, she made plans to enter various rehabilitation centres, went into one, left and resumed drug use, became pregnant, was admitted to hospital to be detoxified, left and resumed drug use. Helen was pregnant when I first met her and making strenuous efforts to stay off drugs. In the last chapter she recounted those efforts both before and after the birth of her child. She was still using when we last met.

Sandra was trying to cut down her consumption of drugs when we first met. She tried several times to stop completely. Twice she went into a drug rehabilitation centre. She was still using when we last met. Anne came to her mother's home to go through withdrawals, determined to stop completely. She managed to stay off drugs for several weeks, but eventually returned to using drugs. Frances was using when we met. Twice she tried to give up, her resolve lasting only a few days each time. She was still using when we last met.

These examples confirm the findings of other studies that com-

---

[1] See Marsh and Simpson (1986), Murphy *et al.* (1989), Oppenheimer *et al.* (1988), Parker *et al.* (1988), Pearson (1987*a*), Stimson and Oppenheimer (1982).

ing off and going back onto drugs is an integral part of the lives of drug users (Brown *et al.*, 1971; Parker *et al.*, 1988; Pearson, 1987*a*; Robertson, 1987; Stewart, 1987; Waldorf, 1970), a finding confirmed by the women themselves:

See when it was 1986 I used to say, 'Don't have a fix in eighty-six', but I did. I've been in a rehab once every year since aboot 1983. At least once every year I've been in somewhere even if it's only been for two days or two months.   (Michelle)

I've been aff it mair in the past five year than I've been on it . . . well roughly the same.   (Sharon)

I've been trying for years to come off.   (Jenny)

Reasons for Wanting to Come Off

The women had a variety of reasons for wanting to come off. None, however, stated that stopping drug use *per se* was a motivating factor. Rather, it was problematic events and circumstances arising out of the lifestyle associated with drug use which provided the impetus to come off.[2] Women sometimes expressed this in general terms of the 'hassles' associated with their way of life:[3]

I just got fed up with the hassles. But I'd still rather have a hit at the New Year than a couple of drinks.   (Rose)

Oh there was too much hassle at everything. People coming to the door and that . . . all the junkies coming to the door.   (Jenny)

One particular 'hassle' was the fear of being caught and sent to prison:

I'm just no' willing to go out and steal. And if I keep that in mind, the jail and things like that, I think I'll be able to do it . . .   (Vicky)

I couldnae handle waking up every morning like that and everything. I mean it was getting to the stage that I didn't see my social worker for my probation so she was going to take me back to court, so if she'd done that she would have taken the kids away and I would have to have gone to jail. And the shoplifting. If I hadn't stopped I would have got caught because they were watching for us coming in every day.   (Donna)

---

[2] For similar findings, see Carlson (1976), Chein *et al.* (1964), Parker *et al.* (1988), Pearson (1987*a*), Stewart (1987).

[3] For similar findings, see Marsh and Simpson (1986), Parker *et al.* (1988), Ray (1964).

I was at court and they saw that I was on probation. The social worker said to me, 'I'll try and get you off but I'm putting it to the judge that I will try to get you into a drug rehab and you'll have to agree to it or else you're gonnae end up in jail'. And I said, 'Aye, OK, I'll go'. That's how I did it the first time. (Sharon).

Besides a growing disenchantment with their way of life, the women's decisions to stop using could be influenced by significant others such as children, family, and partners. Pregnancy, as we saw in the previous chapter, was often regarded both as an opportunity for a new, drug-free beginning and as a condition which called for a mandatory withdrawal from drugs. Having and caring for children was also a powerful incentive, as was the threat of having children removed from the mother's care.[4] In some cases, women attempted to abstain in order to have children restored to their care:

I have to come off now if I want the weans back. I have to prove that I'm responsible enough to look after them.   (Fiona)

I'm determined to get aff them, get a new life and get my wean back. (Diane)

Pressures from parents and partners were also cited as influential:[5]

I went into the rehab for my Ma, it was a case of 'I've no' got a drug problem. I'll just go in here to keep her happy.' That's what it was.   (Louise)

Colin had been in a rehab and told me more or less that if I didnae sort myself out whilst he was sorting himself out there wasn't much point, which I knew myself.   (Rose)

Concern about their health was another major impetus.[6] Women's health can be and is affected in many ways by drug use (Blenheim Project, 1988). Most drug users look undernourished, a result both of a refusal to spend money on food which could otherwise purchase drugs and of the appetite-reducing effect of drug taking (Blenheim Project, 1988; Mondanaro, 1989). When they do purchase food, it is usually junk food, in the form of take-away meals or simply an assorted bag of chocolate and sweets (Kroll, 1986; Morabia *et al.*, 1989). Those who have recently been either in

[4] For similar findings, see Griffiths and Pearson (1988), Hogg (1989), Oppenheimer *et al.* (1988).

[5] For similar findings, see Brown *et al.* (1971), Drug Indicators Project (1989), Ong (1989).

[6] For similar findings, see Brown *et al.* (1971), Marsh and Simpson (1986).

a rehabilitation centre or in prison are easily distinguished from other drug users: they do not look painfully thin. Rather, as appetite returns and with the provision of regular meals, they are plump and well-looking:

I put on a stone in about six days 'cause I was just eating and eating and eating. (Louise)

Usually I'm about six stone. I'm dead proud of myself because I've managed to put on a bit of weight. (Lorraine)

The use of pharmaceutical heroin is not by itself physiologically dangerous (G. Harding, 1988). Most of the health repercussions from use of street heroin arise from the adulterants with which it is cut and from the use of unsterile injecting equipment, facts of which many of the women were aware:

I think you are more likely to do something to your health with the stuff that they cut it with rather than the heroin itself. I've no' really seen anyone, apart from folk who have died, I have no' really seen anyone suffering the effects of heroin. It's mostly suffering the effects of what it is cut with. (Rose)

Indeed, many of the women thought that heroin was a safer drug than some of the other substances they used:

Diconal just snookers your veins. You've no' got a vein in your body with diconal, there's so much chalk in them . . . I've no' got one vein left in my body, not one. If I go oot there and get knocked down, God knows where they are going to get blood from. I havenae got one vein in my body. I've got none in my neck, nowhere. (Lorraine)

I take fits with those jellies, a lot of people take fits. Like they could be sitting here the now and the next thing, bang, they've taken a fit. (Susan)

No matter what the substance, however, unhygienic injecting practices undoubtedly lead to serious health problems. The HIV virus which causes AIDS offers the most serious health risk, from sharing unsterile injecting equipment. Abscesses are common, as is infection with Hepatitis B; there is a risk of septicaemia from using unsterilized needles and syringes; veins collapse from over-use; adulterants can put a strain on the liver, resulting in liver damage (Blenheim Project, 1988). All of these illnesses and their debilitating effects can spur the women to attempt to relinquish drug taking:

I'm waiting on a phone call from the rehab and hopefully I'll be going in this week. I'm going to give it a right good try because other than that I'm going to end up lying dying of AIDS somewhere.   (Lorraine)

I've got cirrhosis of the liver caused first by Hep B and then carrying on with heroin.   (Emma)

I took Hepatitis B and I was in Ruchill Hospital, weighed about five stone, you know like a skeleton, and that was me off it for six month.   (Sally)

I just couldnae handle it anymore. I had hepatitis. I was in Ruchill for about eighteen weeks with malnutrition and all that. I was starving and what I was eating I couldn't keep down. I thought I was going to die.   (Kate)

The reasons discussed so far for wanting to stop drug use, like those cited in other studies, can all be considered as external constraints on the women (Ong, 1989; Parker *et al.*, 1988; Pearson, 1987*a*; Schasre, 1966; Stewart, 1987; Waldorf, 1970). However, such external pressures were regarded by the women as insufficient to guarantee success in their withdrawal from drugs. It was a commonly held belief amongst the drug using community that attempts based on these grounds were doomed to failure. What was lacking was the necessary total commitment, or 'readiness' (Rosenbaum and Murphy, 1984), which was only present when the drug user wanted to stop drugs for her own sake. She needed to feel that this new state of being was what she wanted, she had to be doing it 'for herself':

Now it's just lately that I've said, 'Oh well, I'll need to get my nut together, really and truly need to get my nut together, get my head screwed on. I'm not . . . it was my wee brother's anniversary last week that died of an overdose, he was a year dead—I'm not doing it for him; I'm not doing it for my son; and I'm not doing it for my husband; I'm not doing it for my mother, my father—I'm doing it for myself this time because that's the only way you can do it.   (Lorraine)

I want to come off for my wean's sake, but most of all for myself.   (Anne)

You've got to want to come off it for yourself.   (Judy)

The first two times I went into a drug rehab centre I wasnae going in for me. I was going in for my Ma. I was like that, 'I'll need to dae it for my ma's sake—it's killing her'. But the last time it was for me and I think that's how I stuck it for so long.   (Helen)

I was in a rehab for three-and-a-half months, but I never really had any intention of staying off it. I was just there for the sake of my Ma. But if you don't really want to do it you'll never do it. I mean if it's not for yourself. (Jenny).

It's no' as if I'm here 'cause my wean's been taken aff me or anything, I'm here for me. (Vicky).

I'd just get cut right aff by my family again if I started using or left here or anything. But that's no' the reason I'm staying here. Any other time I've tried it, it's been for them, but this time it's for me. And that's how I think I will get aff it. (Alice)

This belief in self motivation may have been regarded as a necessary ingredient in trying to stop using drugs, but it was not by itself sufficient. In almost all cases (the only exceptions being Alice, who was still in the maternity hospital and drug-free at the end of my fieldwork, and Rose, who was an ex-user of five years when I met her) the women returned sooner or later to their drug habit.

Difficulties in Staying Off

One of the aspects of stopping the use of opiates most commonly assumed to be difficult is the experience of withdrawal symptoms.[7] In Chapter 2, the women described some of the mental and physical symptoms associated with this syndrome and how (for many) this was the first indication of their physical dependence. Coming off drugs means that this state has to be faced:

I wasnae getting like pains and that. I was going through a different withdrawal. It's more craving I was going through and that is bad as well . . . The craving got me more than anything else. It drives me mad. See when . . . if I hear a lot of people just talking about drugs, I go out of their road 'cause I hate to start maybe thinking about some jellies 'cause you're dying for it after it. (Alice)

On Anne's third day of withdrawal, she too found the craving and mental symptoms difficult to bear:

I'm all agitated still and my legs and back are killing me. I thought it got better after three days, everyone I know says the third day is the worst. I haven't slept for the last three days and it's murder being by yourself. I can't think of anything else but drugs—last night I saw some paper with

---

[7] See Griffiths and Pearson (1988), Lindesmith (1968), Robertson (1987), Schasre (1966).

something white on it and thought it was smack. I thought 'What's my Ma doing with smack?' Do you know what it was? Polyfilla.   (Anne)

However, in line with the findings of recent studies (Parker *et al.*, 1988; Pearson, 1987*a*; Stewart, 1987), whilst none of the women enjoyed the experience, it was not regarded as a deterrent as great as other aspects of a drug-free existence.

The longest I've ever seen anybody withdrawing was about ten days. But it's no' the actual withdrawing, it's the way you cannae sleep and your mind is going all the time. The funny thing is that see after about two weeks to three weeks you think you are cured. But you're no'. That's just the start of your recovery. That is really the start of the hard times to come.   (Rose)

It's easy to come off drugs but it's no' easy to stay aff them. Because it is easy. You can come off it in a week, the problem is staying off it for the rest of your life. In six years time I'll still have that urge but it will not be as strong as it is the noo. You'll always have that urge, same as if you stop smoking.   (Louise)

Like drug users in recent studies (Parker *et al.*, 1988; Pearson, 1987*a*, 1987*b*; Stewart, 1987), all the women claimed that the lifestyle which surrounded drug use made it difficult to stick to a drug-free existence. This was due to two main factors. First, by the time most of the women made their first attempt to come off, their social support and friendship networks consisted mainly of other drug users. Observing others using drugs was a temptation most found hard to resist, particularly if their partner continued consumption. To avoid such temptation, loneliness and social isolation had to be endured. Secondly, not only was drug taking suspended, but also all the activities that accompanied this. Restructuring of time became a problem. Both of these aspects assumed immense proportions, and contributed more to resumption of drug use than the withdrawal symptoms which result when drug taking ceases.

If I want to come off I'll need to get away from here—oh yes I'll need to get away. I mean you walk down the arcade and they know you've been a junkie and they offer you stuff.   (Liz)

See when I came oot of the hospital and I was going doon the arcade everybody was like that to me, 'Looking for kit, looking for tems?'   (Kate)

I had been thinking about coming off for a while and I thought if I could go to college it would give me something to do and that would help me. But the first class I walked into a lassie I knew was there and she was a dealer. I was like that, 'Oh God!' And it was a case of going up for a bit off her every day. Because she was a friend she would give me turn-ons.   (Rose)

I keep going back to it and all that. But it is like . . . see passing junkies in the street, I used to be . . . when I did come off it, people used to think I was weird because I would pass them in the street or just say 'Hi'. And then when I did start talking to them that's when I'd start to go downhill again. 'Cause that is one thing you can't do with junkies 'cause they want to fill you in on who's got things and what's going on. So you can't do it, you've got to keep back from them. Definitely.   (Jenny)

A lot of junkies are jealous because somebody's aff it and they've no' got the guts to go and admit they've got a drug problem and want to try and get aff it so a lot of it is to do with jealousy. They don't want to see you doing well so they'll offer you drugs to get you back to the way you used to be and then you'll no' be any better than them. I've done it. I've seen people that have been aff and I've offered them it because I've been jealous of them. I didnae want people that used to be the same as me better than me because they've come aff it. It's surprising the amount of times they'll say, 'Oh aye, I'll take a hit'. They'll end up taking a hit and before you know it they're junkied up again.   (Louise)

I'm afraid to go out down that arcade 'cause I know I'll get offered stuff (Anne)

Anne had managed to stay off drugs for about three weeks when she made this remark. During this time she had been staying with her mother and had not left the house, for fear of temptation. A few days later she reported feeling stronger and able at least to think about venturing outside. She decided to attend a meeting in the local drug project. A group had been set up there by drug users for drug users. Although it was mainly intended for those who were not consuming drugs, there was no bar on present users from attending. Indeed, the meeting was a forum in which difficulties in abstaining could be discussed and pressure put upon those still using to consider stopping. Anne felt she could benefit at this stage from the support of such a gathering. The meeting, however, was not a success:

Angela and Lynne were both full of it and there's nothing worse than seeing someone who's like that. I felt like going for a hit. And that Lynne, she was punting kit. She actually had the kit on her. Telling us she was going out to sell it. I felt like killing her.   (Anne)

Anne managed to resist the temptation put in her way by her peers, but a few weeks later her husband came out of prison and within a short time she had resumed her drug habit.

Relationship with a drug using partner can seriously jeopardize the resolve to give up drug taking (Farkas, 1976; Kaufman, 1985; Parker *et al.*, 1988; Smithberg and Westermeyer, 1985; Stewart, 1987), unless that resolve is undertaken at the same time and with the same degree of commitment (Pearson, 1987*a*; Stewart, 1987):

Aboot six weeks ago Stephen started using every day and I said to him that he was really putting me under pressure, because I couldnae handle it, watching him using all the time. He understood that and since then we've just been taking maybe one a week or sometimes two and sometimes don't take anything at all.   (Helen)

I think it is impossible for somebody that has a junk problem to come off it if they are living with someone that's using. 'Cause the temptation is too much there all the time around them. Plus the way of life. I mean you couldnae live a different way of life if your partner was living the same life 'cause you are bound to get involved and I don't think it is possible I really don't.   (Rose)

I always seem to do better on my own without Andrew.   (Kate)

There is always one that doesnae want to come off. I think it is . . . one pulls the other down. There is hardly ever a time when the two of them want to come off. One says it and the other will agree but it's because they're full of it at the time.   (Vicky)

He was up at the hoose today and doing my nut in 'cause he's still using. I'm feeling brilliant 'til he comes up.   (Sharon)

For some women, the answer to the problem created by others around them using was to seek out a drug-free environment. This usually meant entering a rehabilitation centre. But even here temptation was still to be found:

When I went in there on Thursday I was determined to come off it. I went in and there were eight people in it. Eight drug users, and six drug users were using drugs and selling them. Now how can you get better in a place like that? I was excited going in. I'd plans about what I was going to do. I was going to go out and get a job and going to do this and going to do that. Then I go in and the next morning, I was going in to get washed and someone said, 'Do you want any tems? No? Oh, are you not into tems? Then I can get you a bit of smack.' I mean no drug user . . . it's like an alcoholic. If there's seven people, say there's eight alcoholics sitting and seven are drunk do you think one is going to stay sober? Under no circumstance! And that is the way it is for drug users.   (Lorraine)

Those who were serious about coming off drugs, no matter how short or transient that intention, felt anger towards those who abused the rehabilitation centres. Drug taking in such places could result in the house being closed down unless the transgressors owned up. The fear of this happening whilst an individual was still undergoing withdrawals or in a state of weak resolve caused resentment towards the culprits. It could also cause some to break the normal rule of not 'grassing' on each other:

I tell people, 'If you want to use drugs, it's no' in here. Use them elsewhere, don't use them here.' And I tell them. I tell them to their face, 'If you are using drugs, I'll stick you in in a minute. 'Cause the place is not going to get shut down for you using, when there are more junkies got to come after us.' And I'm branded a grass as soon as people walk in here, but I don't care. I let them know. I don't hide it from them. I'm like that, 'If you are no' here to get off, what are you here for?' 'Cause the place will eventually get shut down if people use all the time.   (Jenny)

Grassing, however, was used more as a threat to encourage people to own up when staff in the centre suspected that drugs were being used and threatened to close the place down. This had almost happened the evening before a visit I made to a centre to see some of the women. One of them had left the previous evening with another female resident, both having admitted to using drugs. They had initially denied this; only the pressures brought to bear on them by fellow residents made them finally confess. The scars of the previous evening's happenings were still visible on the remaining women:

They were trying to cover up and say they weren't. But we are all junkies, we all know. We all know as soon as somebody is full of it. See like the other night, there was a lot of panic in this house. There was people who had nowhere to go. Like Marion. Her Ma and that not knowing about her, and there were really a lot of things. There is the staff shouting, 'There's more people in the house who know who is using and won't say'. I said it in the house meeting. Everybody was thinking it, but nobody was bold enough to say it. The first one I pulled out was Michelle. But I think Michelle thought it was just me getting back at her, being snide to her. But I wasn't. It was just that everybody thought it and nobody was saying it to them. So I had to say it. I had to be the one to pull it out of them. So I said to Michelle and she just pure point-blank denied it. Defences were up right away. And that's the first thing we do. I mean all junkies just put up their defences straight away. She'd just as well have admitted it, with all her defences going up. And that was the first house meeting. So the next house meeting again, there was still drugs in the house. Somebody else using in the house and they're no' admitting it. Nobody would still say the name. And I went, 'Marie, they are getting at you'. And she just kind of said, 'What do you mean?' I went, 'Don't tell me what do you mean. You have been jaggin' for the past few days in here.' And she was like that, 'No, I've no', I've no''. I went, 'Aye you have Marie'. (Jenny)

I was terrified when I thought the house was going to get shut down, 'cause I know I'd have been using that night, 'cause I'm no' long enough . . . I'm no' strong enough yet, or long enough aff it. I was terrified. I had they butterflies in me, you know that scared feeling. I honestly did have, 'cause I was like that, 'If I get out here again the now, that's me, I'm not going to try again'. So I was terrified . . . and they're going about fuckin' dancin' and singin'. They're no giving a fuck if they get discharged, they made that quite clear. (Marion)

I was ragin', know what I mean? I was really beelin', but they werenae giving a fuck. I was ragin' . . . that's . . . it annoyed me, 'cause I was jealous an' all. Truthfully I was. And that's me being honest with myself. I'm not kidding myself on, saying, 'Och, I could walk out of here and stay aff it'. This is my first time straight in the past two-and-a half year. The first time I've ever experienced a full set of withdrawals and the first time I've stayed aff it for so long but I still don't feel strong enough to go anywhere there's drugs. I think if anybody was to offer me them, it'd be like a wee devil and a wee angel sitting on tap of my heid saying, take it, no don't take it. I know it would. And when there was a chance that the house was going to get shut down last night, I shat myself. I would have taken a hit last night if I had got put out of here. I would just have gone right up the road for eggs or some-thing. But I really want to come off it and I'm not abusing drugs so I'm no' walking out of here for somebody else's use of drugs. Those that are using can own up and leave instead of the whole hoose getting shut 'cause there's people in here really trying. I knew for a fact that I would lose everything if this place got shut down and that is why I was dead angry with the residents that had taken drugs. (Diane)

Treatment

Seeking help in a rehabilitation centre, then, had its own inbuilt hazards. Despite this, however, the women were often full of praise for the support they received there, seeing the staff as dedicated to their work:

I mean the staff work like slaves. They are slaving themselves all the time here. They are here from morning right through to midnight. They put in hundreds of effort to help us. (Jenny)

I mean this place, they're trying to shut it up and that man [the leader] had put so much into this place and helped me personally.   (Lorraine)

The staff gie us a lot of leeway and our outings and things like that. I mean if we say we want to go somewhere they'll take us or we'll get a compromise ... I mean they're dead good with us. If you want to bake they'll let you bake. It's really good and they get videos out and all that. It is a good house. It's the best rehab I've been in. I've only been in two, but what I've heard about some others, I don't fancy. People I know that's been in them. It's mair or less like—they get a reputation of just a junkie hotel. You go in there and every three or four weeks or something the house gets shut down because everybody's using in it. But this place has got a glowing reputation outside so it has.   (Louise)

This place is good. All the residents are brand new. When you come in you get some welcome.   (Alice)

I like it here—well I don't like *being* here but it's ... I think it's good. You know that there's folks here. I mean listening to other junkies. It is one of the best ones out.   (Vicky)

Not everyone either wanted to or was able to find a place in a centre. Residential places are few in comparison to the numbers of drug users seeking such a place at any one time. Some women, of course, did not have a choice. Those with children often found it impossible to consider a drug rehabilitation centre. Without family support, going into a rehabilitation centre which did not cater for children would also mean putting their children into care and therefore put them at risk of losing their children if their attempt at staying drug-free failed. Caring for children, as well as fear that they would be taken into care if the mother admitted to having a drug problem, was therefore a disincentive for some mothers to seek treatment.[8] At the same time, the thought of going through withdrawals at home whilst caring for a young child was a daunting thought, putting the women in an impossible predicament:

I know it will be hard, but I can't leave her. I've tried it before. I went into one rehab and left after a couple of days, heartbroken. I went into another and came out after four days, heartbroken. Nobody can understand the way you feel. The wean means everything to me. When I was using really heavy I wouldn't let her out of my sight—that's how it gets you.   (Frances)

---

[8] Other studies which have also found that fear of losing children is a disincentive to seek help include Colten (1982), Dorn and South (1985), Hartnoll and Power (1989), Hogg (1989), Mondanaro (1989), Reed (1985). Studies which have found that caring for children makes help-seeking difficult include Mondanaro (1989), Prather (1981), Reed (1985), Stewart (1987), Wolfson and Murray (1986).

Women should come off with their children around them because coming off means having to deal with emotions which have been suppressed. It's like learning what your children are like all over again. It's learning what you yourself are like again—you're a different person. But women need support during this time. What we need are more places for women to go in with their weans to come off.   (Rose)

Not all women agreed with Rose, however. Fiona had had her children taken into care because of her drug use. She knew that, at the forthcoming children's hearing to discuss the custody of the children, it would help her case if she was receiving treatment. The problem was that she considered that it would be best for her to move away from her environment completely for a while, perhaps seeking a place in a rehabilitation centre in England. She did not feel that she could cope with children and come off drugs at the same time, so did not want to take them with her. Going far away from her home, however, would have meant that she would not have ready access to her children, a factor in her disfavour when the children's custody would be decided. Fiona decided to stay at home—a decision which, as we saw at the end of the last chapter, neither helped her to stop her drug use nor gain custody of her children.

Laura also wanted to stop her drug use. She had a child and a part-time job, was coping well with both and did not want to lose them. Her drug use, however, was beginning to escalate, and she was beginning to experience problems in financing it. She did not want to jeopardize her custody of her child by turning to shoplifting or prostitution. She did not want to go into a drug rehabilitation centre because her mother was the only person with whom she could leave the child. Her mother, however, did not know that she was a drug user and Laura did not want her to know. She did not want to lose her child by putting the child into care. Her friend was being maintained on a methadone prescription. In Glasgow, methadone was prescribed only sparingly, often to those with the HIV virus or to help others with high-risk activities to change their behaviour and reduce the risk to which they were exposing themselves. Laura thought that she was a good candidate to be helped, and asked her friend if she could accompany her on her next visit to the methadone clinic. She came back incensed at the attitude she had encountered:

I'm too good, too good for a junkie. I was talking to this woman for about one-and-a-quarter hours. She asked me how long I'd been using—since I was fifteen I told her—how many times I'd tried to come off it; what I used; who I'd slept with; if I'd shared works. I told her that I'd used Cath's works and I'd slept with a guy without using a condom—that's not true but I just said it and that if I could do it once I could do it again. But she said I was just too good to be true, too good to be a junkie because I've kept my house together, looked after my wean, kept my job. I even told her that it would kill my mother if she knew. I even told her that I sometimes go shoplifting—not often but when I do the first thing I think about is my mother and how she'd die if I got caught. But no—just because I keep myself clean, change my underwear, wash myself. Just because I'm not a prostitute, because I don't sleep with everybody, because I don't go up the town to get money, I don't get my wee bottle of methadone. It's just not fair. If I went back next week and told her that I was a prostitute I'd get it . . . I just wanted them to cut me down. At least that way I wouldnae be scratching around for money every day. I mean I know it's our own fault— nobody forced us into taking it—I know lots of people that took it but it wasn't that, I wanted to take it—but I'm trying my best and all I want is a bit of help. But nobody wants to know—not my GP, not the hospital, nobody, because I'm too good to be a junkie.

Vicky spoke of the vicious circle surrounding women with children who do seek residential treatment:

I got a place in a rehab, but before I went in I had to find someone to watch the wean. But my Ma drinks and my Da had just died a couple of months before and she was hitting the bottle. So I said to my health visitor, who'd got me the place, 'I don't think I'll be able to go in, I've got nobody to look after the wean'. And she came doon on me like a ton of bricks and said, 'Oh well that's it, we'll just have to put the wean into foster care'. Oh, and I just hit the roof and I started greetin' and swearin'. And she said, 'That's the only thing. If you don't go into the rehab you're just going to get worse and it's no' good for the wean'. And the only reason I had told her in the first place was so that she could pull a few strings to get the wean into nursery school and at that time she had got me an appointment at a drug clinic but I didnae go—I didnae want aff at that time only to get the wean a nursery place. So what she was saying was, 'You're at it again'. But what happened was that my Ma heard about me going into this place and she sobered up and she got her into another nursery school near where she lives. But the head teacher at the old nursery said to my Ma, 'Tell her we'll keep the place open for the wean until she comes back. But tell her that if she does bring her back and I sense any drugs in her I'll just have to phone the social services. I'll not give her another chance.'   (Vicky)

Genuine difficulties encounterd by drug using mothers can there- fore be seen as excuses to avoid treatment rather than as the result of concern for their children.

For a time, one of the rehabilitation centres had experimented with allowing children to come with their mother, but here too the mother's ability to prove she could care for her child was put in jeopardy:

No more children are allowed now . . . I think there was too much hassle because they've got to go to the children's panel and prove that they're going to be looked after in here and it's not good for the weans being in a house full of junkies and seeing people coming in and maybe people are being put out for bringing stuff in with them and it was a lot of hassle for some lassies having to prove that their weans were being looked after. Some people just werenae willing to give you a chance to do that.   (Donna)

The difficulties involved in reconciling the interests of children and the desire to cease drug use led some mothers to attempt to come off in the community. Joanne had no support where she lived to help her look after her five-year-old son, and had come to her mother's house to go through her withdrawals and be assured that the child would be looked after. The child had recently started school, and the journey to school entailed an hour's journey on two buses. Joanne decided that the most practical solution was to keep the child home from school for a week, by which time she thought she would be physically strong enough to undertake the journey every day. Her mother disagreed, and wanted the child to be transferred to the local school. During Joanne's first week of abstention, this subject was a constant source of anxiety to her:

My ma wants me to change him to the school here but I don't think that's best for him. I think it would just upset him to change so soon after starting and then have to change back again when we go back home. But my Ma doesnae see it like that. She thinks I'm just being selfish. She thinks all I've got to do is to make up my mind to it and I'll stop. But I'm doing my best for him by coming here to come off. It's no' what's best for me.

Joanne's recovery from both her physical and her mental withdrawals took longer than she expected. About ten days later, she decided to transfer the child to the local school near her mother's house. In this move she had the support of her social worker. For the next two months she and the child continued to stay with her mother. For most of this time, Joanne remained drug-free. She moved back home but remained in touch. It was soon apparent that her drug use had started again, although she denied this, a fact which incensed her drug using friends:

Sitting there scratching, saying she was allergic to her tights. I felt like saying to her, 'Have you got tights on your arms as well then?'   (Liz)

Aye, and wiping up the table and tidying everything away. That's a dead giveaway. Does she think we're daft?   (Lynne)

Spending time in the company of drug users, I soon became aware of two facets of the behaviour of those heavily under the influence of drugs. The first is that drug users scratch themselves a lot (a result of the adulterants in heroin in the bloodstream). The second factor is an excessive and compulsive tidying and clearing away of anything lying around.[9] Joanne had displayed both these behaviours on this particular occasion. But Joanne's verbal concealment of her renewed habit was not because she questioned the perception or intelligence of her friends; it resulted from her fear that her children, newly removed from the 'at risk' register, would be returned to it if it became known that she was using, and she would once again come under the scrutiny of social workers.

The drug using mother, then, has hurdles to overcome in that she has to take into account, when seeking help, the effect this will have on her children and, in addition, the risk she is undertaking that she may lose custody of her children by admitting that she has a drug problem which requires help.

When women did seek treatment or help, besides the problems occasioned by the presence of children, they were often disappointed at the quality of help offered to them. The most frequent complaint was the lack of understanding of the needs and feelings of drug users:

The first time I seriously tried to come off I signed myself into a psychiatric hospital for three weeks. That was a waste of time. That was just talking to a psychiatrist and just telling the psychiatrist what I think he wanted to hear so that he'd fill me full of Largactil and it was just nae ... it just wasnae the answer ... I mean it sounds daft but the last thing you want to talk about when you are coming off is junk. You are trying not to think about it. I found that doctors, when you go to them for help for addiction, all they are interested in is what you use, how much you use, when you use. It is not to help you, it is to increase their own understanding ... Plus I don't think that it's the right time when you are just coming off to maybe talk to someone like a psychiatrist because you are so confused and things are going to be bad for you. You have got that high and low and high and

---

[9] For similar findings, see Stewart (1987).

low . . . I think that the best way to come off is cold turkey, apart from if it's things like downers you're coming off because you could have fits that way. If it's just heroin I think the best way is to get your system cleared out as quick as possible and suffer the withdrawals. And then, get a bit of peace and quiet and if possible away from the environment.   (Rose)

I didnae like being near they day centres . . . it wasnae during the day that bothered me anyway. It was at night. And I didnae fancy some of those counsellors. They were dead, dead, nice people but just didnae have a clue. (Vicky)

When I went to my doctor's to get help I was the first drug addict my doctor had ever had. That is where I went at first, to my doctor's and he sent me to a psychiatrist. I said, 'I don't think I need a psychiatrist, I need help. I need someone to help me get off the drugs.' He said, 'But the psychiatrist will tell you why you took drugs in the first place'. 'But I know why I took them in the first place. It was out of curiosity. I wanted to try it.' I knew there were residential places and I was hoping to get in somewhere and get off drugs. And he was wanting to send me to a psychiatrist! I cracked up. (Jenny)

Some types of help were more appreciated, particularly those in which understanding rather than condemnation were on offer. We have already heard some of the positive feelings towards the staff in residential centres. One other praised service was that provided by the detached drug workers in the area. The particular attraction of this service for the women was that they did not need to be deceitful or manipulative to attain what they wanted. Many drug users often want help with the practical problems arising from their drug use without necessarily wanting to cease use of drugs. The lack of understanding of this by many workers in the drug field means that a pretence of the desire to abstain has to be proffered:

It's always the drug worker I go to for any problem, not just drugs . . . One day we were in the community centre and my sister and her man were up from London and I said to him, 'I'll be back in five minutes, I'll need to try and catch this guy for a bit of smack'. My sister said, 'Christ, she's just said that in front of a social worker'. I was like that, 'He's cool. He's not like that. He knows I use and that's it. What's the use of telling lies.' I have telt him lies in the street to save myself getting into a heavy conversation at a street corner with him. I've said to him the next day that I didnae want to tell him such and such because somebody or other was around at the time. I just tell him the truth. I can tell him anything. It's as if he's learnt about the job. A lot of them go into the job to learn and I think he's learnt it first and he's oot amongst us all—he's not stuck in an office somewhere. He's doon in among the drug scene every day, practically, and I've seen him helping people rather than hindering them and just being there. I've seen him doing practical help. Going to prisons and hospitals and that. He has *helped* . . . When I went to see one of the top doctors in drug abuse a few years ago, I was in his office for thirty-five minutes and he sat and looked at a wall and never said a word. Not one word. He looked at his watch and said, 'Time's up', and I had to walk oot the door. Never said a thing, just to see if I would go all rubber or whatever. But we had been told his tactics by other people: 'He did this to me and he did that to me, so he'll do it to you.' So you know what to say or do to get your script at the end of it . . . You learn to behave in the way they want you to. It's conditional.   (Kate)

Most women realized, however, that to come off, other factors, rather than the type of help that was available, were important:

At the end of the day you can only get so much help and advice and encouragement. At the end of the day it is up to you whether you are gonnae take it and use it and deep down inside it is up to you.   (Sharon)

There's no solution to stop people taking drugs, not unless they want to come off.   (Rose)

This is not to say that drug treatment centres of whatever sort were not helpful. They were regarded more as places where the women could go to to sort out immediate problems, or to seek refuge when 'hassles' were becoming overwhelming. To quit drug use completely, however, some other obstacles had to be overcome.

More Difficulties in Coming Off

It's not the hits it's just all the circumstances.   (Kate)

The beginning of this chapter set out the women's perceptions of the difficulties and temptations posed by the presence of drug using companions when attempting to come off drugs. By this stage in their drug careers most of their friends are drug users, and they have come to identify most closely with them. Giving up drugs, whether in a residential setting or at home, means that these friends must be avoided. This in turn entails a period of loneliness:

What worries me is being lonely again when I go outside. In here you've got people round about you. But that is my worst fear in leaving here, being lonely again when I get a house outside. Will I go back to drugs? I just couldn't leave here and have nothing to do 'cause I would be back in the darts team within an hour.   (Jenny)

I can't handle being off and living on my own.   (Kate)

A further difficulty involved in spending time by oneself and being straight is the amount of time the drug user has to think. Many of the thoughts at this time are unpleasant, making a return to drug use and the possibility of blocking out such thoughts very attractive. One of the attractions of drug taking was the lack of emotion experienced whilst under the influence of drugs.

On drugs you have no feelings.   (Kate)

It's the ultimate escape.   (Helen)

You've no' got feelings . . . Well you have got feelings but you're no' in touch with them.   (Jenny)

Coming off drugs meant coming to terms with these suppressed emotions, and brought the women face to face with feelings they did not want and past experiences that they would rather have forgotten. Guilt for actions carried out when using drugs was one of the most difficult emotions that the women experienced:

Sometimes when I've been off for a while and I start to feel good, I feel guilty about all the things I've done especially to my Ma and Da.   (Sharon)

It is only when you are straight for a wee while that you realize . . . you feel terrible . . . 'cause it takes a while to get in contact with your feelings. With me it was the wean. That she has missed out . . . well I've missed out on the wean growing up. I really missed her growing up. Just there the past few months that I have been straight that I have realized . . . and I don't share needles noo 'cause I've got the virus, except for once. One lassie wanted to use my works and I didnae want her to but she was like that, 'Please, please'. I made sure she put bleach through them before she used them. But that's no' saying that she's no' going to get it, but she was really desperate. But I still think, now that I'm straight, I wonder if that lassie has got anything off me. It is a thing you've got to live with, I'll never know . . . But I still think maybe I've gave her it and then she's given it to other people.   (Jenny)

What I'm coping with now, I'm no' coping with a drug problem, it's the emotional side of it. Like my Da's been dead for four year—about three weeks ago it all came back to me and I realized that my Da was dead. And I thought, 'God, I miss him'—but for four year I've blocked it oot, so now I'm starting to cope with his death. And like the abortion, after the abortion I was jaggin' again so now I'm coping with the effects of getting rid of the wean. That's two things I've got to cope with. I didnae know what was involved in coming off drugs. I thought, 'Och, you just get over your strung ootness and that's you'. There's a lot mair to it than that. Getting over the physical side of it is nothing but then you've got the mental side and that is the hardest part . . . The biggest feeling you have when you come aff it is guilt for what you've done to everyone like your Ma, close friends and relatives—because I'd've taken the eyes oot o' my Ma's heid if I thought I could get a score deal for them. So what you dae to them you feel really, really guilty about. It's like a delayed reaction because when you're using drugs you're no' thinking about it. If you run away and start using again then you could use for five years and as soon as you come off it in five years time then it's still going to be there . . . so facing up to it the now is better and that's how if I say I'm going for a hit I say to myself, 'That's not going to do you any good, you're going to have to face up to it when you come off it again'.   (Louise)

Unfortunately Louise did not stick to her resolution; a few weeks after this conversation she was out of the rehabilitation centre and back on drugs.

Once the props of their drug lives had gone, besides the feelings of guilt they experienced, the women also found themselves lacking the confidence necessary to cope with a new way of life:

It's no' the drugs that's the problem, it's me. I've got no confidence . . . I've never had a job . . . although I don't think I'm stupid. I think that I could do something . . . I don't know if it is a personal thing, but confidence is a killer. You know being a drug addict. I mean you are as good as the person next to you walking along the street, but you don't feel it. I mean and you are. But it is hard to . . . I don't know . . .   (Sharon)

Using gives you confidence, without it I'm dead shy, embarrassed, everything like that.   (Jenny)

Only one woman had managed to come off and stay off drugs. Rose had been drug-free for five years after being a drug user for seven. She described problems in her successful attempt to come off similar to those facing women who were still trying to achieve success:

The funny thing is that see after about two weeks to three weeks you think you are cured. I mean you are like that, 'I'm never going to use again, I'm cured'. But you're no'. Do you know what I mean? That's just the start of your recovery. After three weeks when your head starts thinking a bit straighter, that is just really the start of the hard times to come. The first three weeks are nothing compared to what is to come if you follow it through because there's all the uncertainties. And everyone thinks 'cause you are over withdrawals and you don't need a hit that you should be all right. But I don't think so many people understand that that's when it really starts getting frightening. You know—'Can I do this?' You've got no confidence in yourself. You don't think you are ever going to be able to manage it. Because you wake up still wanting a hit, you maybe don't need it, but you still want it, you feel a failure and . . . It is just really really hard. And then you start getting extremes of emotions and you wonder, 'Is it worth it? Why am I doing this?' And then that's when I think you need people to talk to. I think at first what you need mostly is people who can help you sort of like going through the horrible withdrawals and all this and that and . . . but it is after that when people don't really want to be involved that you need people. As I says, you think oh you don't need a hit any more, you're all right. You maybe look OK on the outside and starting to put on weight and looking after your appearance a bit better. But it is then . . . I was really terrified, I was frightened. I thought I was gonnae be in the rehab forever because I wouldnae be able to come back, wouldnae be able to do anything. Felt stupid, you know, I really felt so thick. A simple thing like writing a letter I just couldnae do it. Talking to people, I couldnae hold a conversation. I was just so frightened about 'Am I doing the right thing?' Because if you've lived one kind of lifestyle you don't think there is any way you could possibly live a straight lifestyle.

One of the most important reasons why the women found it difficult to avoid involvement with drugs was that, as Rose has indicated, they had nothing to replace the routine associated with their drug use. Despite its chaotic appearance to outsiders, the drug user's life is structured and organized. They have to be at certain places at certain times, they have to organize fund-raising. As for others in different walks of life (the unemployed, the retired), when that routine is disrupted, the restructuring of time can prove difficult:[10]

When I came off I didnae know what to do with myself. I used to want to go out shoplifting. Sometimes I would do a big ironing instead. I never used to do that, I just used to iron the clothes that I was going to wear that day before going out shoplifting.   (Liz)

It's really hard to pass the time when you're off it. Sometimes I was that bored I'd think to myself, 'I'll go out shoplifting'. You're really busy when you're using—up in the morning, out graftin', then back to sell the stuff and then looking for drugs—that can take hours.   (Linda)

---

[10] For further discussion, see Jahoda (1982), Pearson (1987a, 1987b), Roth (1963).

When you're using, it's the same routine every day. Once you break that routine, then you will have nothing to do. You'll have all this time on your hands. (Louise)

Aware of this, Louise had spent her time in the rehabilitation centre, before returning to drug use, in planning what she would do when she left:

If you get things organised while you're in a rehab then you'll find that you do have things to do. I'm going to do a typing course and once I've done that I will try to get a job with my qualification. And I'm going to do voluntary work with SAM [*Scottish Aids Monitor, a voluntary organization set up to provide help for those who are HIV positive or have AIDS*] and that will keep me going at night. Or if you go to college you'll have studying to do at night or if you arrange voluntary work you can do that. You can do some voluntary work during the day and that's taking up a couple of days, then you can have some at night and that's taking up a couple of nights. You can go and visit your family or you can visit the rehab you used to be in. There's never a shortage of things to do. It's just getting yourself to get up to get it all arranged. If you dae that then you'll no' find yourself bored and if you fill you're time then as time goes by you'll find you don't think about going for a hit because you've got all this activity to dae and at night you're just bushed and you're wanting to go to your bed. But if you sit and do nothing then you will just end up going back on it.   (Louise)

Other women, too, talked about what they would like to help them stay off:

I would like to get a job for comimg oot so's I could just . . . that would pass the time. Well you're working to what—five o'clock and then I'm up early in the mornings, surely I'll be tired at night and just watch the telly and . . . just try and get into the routine of leading a normal life. That's all I want. (Alice)

All I want is a wee hoose somewhere away from here for me, the wean and my boyfriend. Just to be straight. Just to be happy wi' oorselves and the wean. (Sharon)

But they had no illusions about the difficulties this entailed:

But I mean it'll be hard to do it, get away and get a hoose. I mean you cannae do much without money.   (Sharon)

But it's . . . whether I'll dae it—and the jobs, it's right hard to get a job . . . I sometimes sit and dream aboot getting a job and then I say to myself, 'Who are you kidding?'   (Alice)

Coming off drugs, then, is a complex procedure. It is not simply a case of making a decision not to consume particular substances. It is a process of decision-making based on a whole series of push-and-pull factors; some encouraging the women to want to quit, others pulling them back. Most of all, coming off entails establishing a whole new way of life and a new set of friends and companions. It was these issues which created and sustained the difficulties the women encountered in their endeavours. Few of the women talked with much enthusiasm about a new way of life. When they talked about restructuring time, they indicated that such restructuring would not be undertaken for the intrinsic interest of another lifestyle, but merely as a way of filling time, of getting through one day and on to another: a bleak prospect which most rejected. Few had any hopeful prospects about the kind of lifestyle they would have in the straight world. Even Rose, who had managed to change her lifestyle, was not totally enamoured of her new way of life:

For the first months you pat yourself on the back because you've managed to stay off but then you begin to ask yourself 'So what? What do I do next?' I still think there must be more to life than this—getting up, getting through the day and going to bed.   (Rose)

Despite their growing disenchantment with their way of life, for most, the straight world held no welcoming beckon:

I'm fed up with this life but at the same time I don't see any way out. It might have been different a few years ago, but now there's nae opportunites—no houses, no jobs, nothing. I've had everything and lost it—there's nothing left. I've lost my family, my wean, nobody wants me. I hate what I do out there on the streets. Yet I cannae face life straight.   (Kate).

It's fuckin' terrible, it wrecks your life and you end up losing everything. You might be sitting there thinking, 'Only one hit, that won't do anything to you'. That's what I thought and that's what everybody else thinks until it happens to you, and it's just terrible, but life without it is just pure borin'. (Helen)

7

Conclusion

The previous chapters have presented an account of the lifestyles of a group of inner-city female intravenous drug users in Glasgow. In particular, they have presented a picture of drug use from the points of view of the women themselves. They have told us how they initially became involved in drug use and how they maintained their drug habit. They have told us about their social interactions, their relationship with their children, and their attitudes towards motherhood. Finally, they talked about their attempts to cease their use of drugs and the difficulties involved in this endeavour. This concluding chapter briefly draws together the main findings and themes which have emerged in the course of the text, drawing comparison, where relevant, with other research.

In the Introduction it was shown that the predominant view of female drug users emanating from most of the literature was that of passive, socially inadequate women who were chaotic, out of control of their own lives, and inadequate, unfit mothers. The findings of this study, however, refute such an image.

The women's active, as opposed to passive, role was emphasized by the women themselves when recalling how they had first begun using drugs. Introduced to drugs through their social networks, none indicated that they had been coerced into drug use; rather, they all proclaimed their willing participation in drug use for reasons such as curiosity, excitement, and the pleasurable effects. Their drug use, rather than the result of submission to male partners' wishes, as many of the studies of female drug use tend to suggest, was often undertaken in the face of opposition from male partners. At each stage on the road to their recognition of physical dependence, the women's active participation was evident, including their move to hard drugs and subsequent move to intravenous use. The women were also active in providing for their own drug use. They raised the finance necessary for their drug purchases, they purchased their own drugs and often performed both functions for their partners, too. Being a drug user entailed a busy, full life for all the women in this study.

Nor was this a life characterized by chaos or lack of control. One striking point about their lives was the structure imposed by providing for a drug habit. They had to be at particular places at particular times to purchase the best deals. They had to organize their revenue-raising activities. Decisions surrounding their drug lifestyle were also taken rationally and pragmatically. In the sphere of drug use itself, the move to injection was undertaken so that the beneficial effects of drugs could be continued in the most economical way possible. Ways of raising money for drugs were similarly thought out in a rational manner. Initially, the easiest and least risky way to raise money was to sell their own possessions. When this stopped being a possibility, the women turned to crime. Here, too, they attempted to reduce the dangers of being apprehended, and subsequently sent to prison, to the best of their ability. Dress was carefully chosen by shoplifters so as not to attract attention from security and other staff in shops. Goods, such as children's clothes, were targeted both because they were fairly easy to steal, being small in bulk, and because they were easy to sell in the community in which they lived. Dealing drugs provided them, not only with funds, but also with a ready supply of drugs for their own use, thus reducing the risks inherent in purchasing drugs.

If apprehended in any of these activities, the penalty was often imprisonment. To reduce the risk of imprisonment another pragmatic decision was taken: they turned to prostitution. Turning to prostitution was not a sign of increasing immorality, as is usually assumed, nor a sign of increasing depravity, but a rational move, in that prostitution, and only prostitution, brought with it ready access to money whilst not attracting a prison sentence following arrest by the police.

Through all these activities, the women became part of a social network of drug users, again refuting the image of female drug users as socially isolated or inadequate. This network provided them with, and enabled them to give, support and advice. It also provided the women with their male partners. At the same time, relationships with the wider society were not severed: the women remained in touch, though less and less frequently, with family and neighbours. It was the negative attitudes of these non-drug users towards drug users, however, which was instrumental in encouraging this gradual detachment, and indirectly fostered strong relationships between the women and other drug users.

One of the strongest images of female drug users is that they are, by definition, unfit mothers. Again, the evidence from the present study shows this to be inaccurate. Most of the mothers in this study looked after and cared for their children perfectly adequately. With regard to motherhood, their attitudes, hopes, and expectations were traditional, and similar to those of non-drug using mothers. When pregnant, most made strenuous efforts to cease their use of drugs out of fear of the harm that drug use might do their baby. However, as in any other sector of society, there were mothers who did not provide care for their children. Some mothers found their drug use, and the lifestyle surrounding it, interfered with their capacity to look after their children. In some cases, such mothers responsibly handed over the care of their children to family members, often their own mothers. A few had had to have their children taken into the care of the social work department. Despite these cases, most mothers were capable mothers and did not fit the stereotype which portrays them as unfit.

The predominant picture of female drug users presented at the beginning of this book does not, therefore, tend to be upheld by the findings of this study. Whilst differing in the ways that they provided for their drug use, the female drug users in this study were all active and involved in the lifestyle which evolved around their use of drugs. In this respect, they resemble more their male counterparts, as depicted in ethnographic studies, rather than the image of drug using women which has previously been presented.

In the Introduction it was shown that the concept of 'career' had been applied in ethnographic studies of male drug users (Feldman, 1968; Fiddle, 1976; Finestone, 1957; Hanson *et al.*, 1985; Hughes *et al.*, 1971; Johnson *et al.*, 1985; Preble and Casey, 1969; Sutter, 1966). Using this concept, the processes involved in entering and maintaining a lifestyle surrounding drug use, as well as the benefits of such a 'career', were uncovered. From these studies the male drug user came to be seen as an active, resourceful person responding in a rational manner to his social circumstances. These social circumstances were often characterized by social deprivation and lack of legitimate career opportunities, similar to the circumstances of the women in this study. The lifestyle associated with drug use allowed these young men to develop an alternative set of activities which provided them with purpose, motivation and status.

Whilst these ethnographic studies were carried out in North America, in Britain the concept of 'career' has similarly been used to explain the rise of the use of heroin amongst young working-class people.[1] Again, in the face of a lack of meaningful activity in the wake of high unemployment, the lifestyle surrounding drug use is seen as conferring on young, mainly male, people the benefits normally associated with paid employment in industrial society. Paid work in our society is a major provider of financial independence, social contacts, participation in a collective purpose, status through the development of skills, self-esteem, and personal identity. It also provides a way of structuring and planning the day, an important feature of life in industrialized society, encouraged in and internalized by us from childhood when 'family and school co-operate . . . to impress on the young . . . the need to fill the day with planned activities' (Jahoda, 1982: 22). The North American and British studies have shown how these benefits can be conferred by a 'career' in drug use, thus making such a lifestyle not only initially attractive, but difficult to relinquish, even when the desire to do so is present, in the absence of alternative, meaningful activity.

Similar benefits derived from their drug using lifestyle were identified by the women in this study. They developed sets of skills which afforded them satisfaction. In the sphere of drug use itself, for example, the skills involved in learning how to inject oneself successfully gave some women great sense of achievement. So, too, did the skills developed in their efforts to raise money. Shoplifting, fraud, dealing in drugs, all require a variety of skills if they are to be carried out successfully. Dealing, for example, requires at least a certain amount of financial acumen in order to maximize profits.

These skills not only provided the women with financial independence but afforded them status within their community. Some women, for example, used their injecting skills to provide an 'injecting service' for those unable to do this for themselves, thus providing for such women a source of finance, whilst at the same time making them important and indispensable in the eyes of other drug users. Similar importance was derived from dealing in drugs. Even within the wider community, their ability to provide poverty-stricken

---

[1] See e.g. Auld *et al.* (1986), Pearson (1987*a*, 1987*b*), Pearson *et al.* (1986).

non-drug users with cheaper goods through the informal economy gave them status and importance.

Their lifestyle also provided them with a source of social contact, and allowed them to be part of a group with whom they shared a common identity and purpose. As we saw earlier in the chapter, it also provided a rigid and habitual structure to their day, organized around the financing and purchasing of drugs.

Indeed, for these women, a career in drug use provided them with conditions not ordinarily encountered in traditional working-class female occupations, even if these had been available to them. Most working-class women's occupations are characterized by low earnings, low status, and lack of skill. The women in this study, on the other hand, had high earnings (otherwise they would have been unable to afford their drugs): they acquired a set of skills which were sought after and which provided them with self-esteem, a social identity, and status. Given the social environment in which these women lived, the likelihood of their finding a career with similar benefits in the formal economy was extremely slight.

However, and again like many male users in other studies, despite the benefits attached to their drug lifestyle, the women all reached a point where they did not wish to pursue this career.[2] The more involved in the drug life they became, the more disadvantages and costs appeared which made them begin to question their commitment to their way of life. The 'hassles' associated with the lifestyle in general—constantly looking for dealers to score from; the risks attached to their ways of making money; health problems arising from the adulterants in drugs, unhygienic injecting practices, and lack of nutritious food as money was kept for drugs; trouble with the police—all eventually began to make the lifestyle associated with drug use less appealing.

One additional cost which faced women to a much greater, if not to an exclusive, extent, arose out of their role in caring for children. The women found that their drug use put caring for their children in jeopardy. In some cases this was a direct consequence of the women's own inability to provide the essential material and emotional requirements for their children because of their escalating drug use. More often, drug use put caring for their children in jeopardy indirectly, through the women's drug use being seen by family

---

[2] See e.g. Pearson (1987*a*, 1987*b*).

as well as professionals as an a priori reason why they were unable to look after their children and therefore should have them removed from their care.

The lifestyle surrounding drug use, therefore, has an additional cost for women. Not only are such women punished through the criminal law, but the presence of children presents a singular method of control of women drug users. As Connors has pointed out, 'the ultimate sanction that a woman may face in the context of drug use is the loss of her child' (1990: 42). In this study, the families of the women, as well as professionals, used the threat of removal of their children to attempt to pressure them into relinquishing their drug use, and thus gave the women an additional reason to want to change their lifestyle.

Yet despite these multiple costs and disadvantages, and despite their wish for a different, drug-free, lifestyle, only one woman had succeeded in stopping her use of drugs for a lengthy period of time. As Gilman has pointed out, many people in legitimate occupations are dissatisfied with their work, but will not give it up until a more attractive option presents itself (Gilman, 1988). To give up work, no matter how unappealing, is to face the detrimental effects of unemployment: loss of identity and status, loss of social contacts, loss of independence, and dislocation of routine time structures. Listening to the accounts of the women, this would seem to be the case for them, too. Giving up the lifestyle to which they had become accustomed, they were faced with loneliness, isolation, and no obvious, meaningful alternative to fill the emptiness left when their way of life was relinquished.

In many ways, then, the career of the inner-city, working-class, female drug user is similar to that of her male counterpart. She becomes involved in drug use for a variety of reasons; she is able and competent in maintaining her drug habit. She derives satisfaction from some of her enterprises, and builds up a way of life around her use of drugs which provides structure and meaning to her day, a structure which she finds difficult to replace when she wants to quit her drug lifestyle.

Yet the control exercised over women through the threat to remove their children highlights a major factor differentiating female and male drug users. Unlike male drug users, female drug users, like many other women, have two careers: one in the public sphere and one in the private, domestic sphere.

Perhaps it is because women have this latter career that the 'alternative career' explanation of drug use has so seldom been applied to women. As this career is always available to women, despite changing economic conditions, and, in the case of motherhood, is 'the chief occupation for which women are raised' (Antonis, 1981: 61), women in general, it could be said, have less need to seek another. Indeed, it could be argued that the existence of this domestic role would make it easier for women to give up a drug using career. In a study of the effects of unemployment in general, Jahoda has argued this point: 'Even if women prefer to have a job, unemployment hits them less hard than men psychologically speaking because an alternative is available to them in the return to the traditional role of housewife that provides some time structure, some sense of purpose, status and activity even though it offers little scope for wider social experiences' (1982: 53). For the women in this study, however, as for many women,[3] a return to the traditional role of housewife was not an acceptable alternative. As we shall see, it was the very existence and conditions of the women's domestic role that was a factor in their continuing drug use.

Various studies have examined motherhood and women's domestic role in general and shown how detrimental this can be for women.[4] Ettore (1989a), for example, argues that 'in the private sphere, women, particularly mothers, have been shown to be the primary emotional copers at potential risk to their physical and mental well being'. The high rate of use of licitly prescribed psychotropics by women has also been linked to the stress of women's domestic lives, and such use has been seen as 'enabling women to maintain themselves in roles they found difficult and intolerable without them'.[5]

In addition to these comments about women's domestic role in general, Carlen has argued that 'the domestic life of Scottish working-class women has traditionally been haunted by the two spectres of slum housing and violent men ... they have also traditionally shouldered the main domestic responsibilities including the paying the bills ... Their domestic position has been one of responsibility without authority or privilege' (1983: 30). She argues that, over the

[3] See e.g. Coyle (1984), Martin and Wallace (1984).

[4] See e.g. Brown and Harris (1978), Ettore (1989a), Graham (1982, 1984).

[5] Cooperstock and Lennard (1979: 335), quoted in Graham (1984: 81). See also Jeffries (1983), London Hospital Women's Group (1976/7) for similar arguments.

centuries, women living in such harsh conditions have learned that alcohol can temporarily deaden the pain caused by such conditions.

Such descriptions succinctly sum up the state of many of the women's domestic lives. Whilst relationships with partners often began out of mutual interest and affection, and were at times characterized by equal participation in their drug careers, as time passed most relationships developed into the traditional dominant male/subordinate female model. With the arrival of children, male partners expected the woman, and only her, to cease drug use. Their displeasure at the woman's inability in many cases to do this, often because of the temptation caused by their partner's continued use, was frequently expressed in the form of violence. Male partners also contributed little in the spheres of child care or domestic activity. Many women, in addition to their domestic duties, also shouldered the bulk of economic responsibilities. Some partners exploited the women's ability to earn money through prostitution, giving up their own earning efforts to live off those of their female partner, a development which the women resented; with the realization that their role had become merely functional in a relationship in which they had expected to be loved, their self-esteem was damaged. Where other women may have turned to licit drugs or alcohol to cope with such harsh realities, the women in this study continued with their use of illicit drugs. Drug use temporarily helped to alleviate and deaden the difficult and often degrading aspects of their relationships with partners. More than this, it provided a form of physical escape to a more meaningful and attractive life outside the home, even when its disadvantages were taken into account.

Motherhood was another aspect of their domestic lives which was a contributory factor in their continuing drug use. Ironically, this arose from the women's traditional attitudes towards motherhood. They expected to, and in most cases did, take on the sole care of their children. Most, as we have seen, were capable, loving, and responsible mothers. However, like many other women, the women in this study did not find, despite expectations to the contrary, that the experience of motherhood fulfilled all their needs. Many found the demands of child care stressful. Studies of motherhood in general have reported other mothers as experiencing feelings of dissatisfaction, tiredness, and depression (Badinter, 1981; Boulton, 1983; Graham, 1984; Graham and McKee, 1980). The incidence of such feelings is higher amongst working-class women, and is associated with poverty, poor housing, and unemployment (Graham, 1984), all conditions characteristic of the women in this study.

Badinter has argued that 'women today express themselves without guilt' when expressing weariness, disillusionment and alienation with regard to motherhood (1981: 313). This may be the case for some, but for many, including the women in this study, disappointment or disillusionment with their role as mothers is experienced as a personal failure—as Christmas has argued, 'the Women's Movement, with its tendency to elitism, has not reached out to our sisters, the junkies' (1978: 858). Like other working-class women, the women in this study did not blame maternity or domesticity for their dissatisfaction (Boulton, 1983). They blamed themselves.

The women had internalized societal expectations that 'a woman can fulfil herself only through motherhood' (Badinter, 1981: 316). The resulting guilt experienced by such women when they discovered this not to be the case was a force underlying the women's drug taking experiences. Similar to other mothers who turn to licitly prescribed tranquillizers as a way of coping with the stress of domestic life, they returned to or increased their use of drugs. For many of the women, drug use became a reward for the drudgery and stress associated with child care. The pursuit of pleasure for women, however, 'makes them feel selfish and unfeminine' (Webster, 1984: 393); thus many women, including those who carry the main responsibility for child care, feel guilty when they desire time for themselves (Antonis, 1981; Silver *et al.*, 1975). The women in this study expressed similar sentiments. Feelings of guilt allowed a vicious circle to be set up in which the women took drugs to cope with their lives and in turn took more to cope with their guilt, guilt further increased if drug use rose to the point where they could no longer care for their child and the child had to be looked after elsewhere.

Drug use for women, at least the women in this study, would seem to have a dual role. As is the case with male users, it provides them in the public sphere with a lifestyle which has meaning, structure, and purpose, gives them an outlet for entrepreneurial and innovative abilities, and provides a form of independence and even equality for women in otherwise subordinate relationships within the domestic sphere. Within this domestic sphere, moreover, drug use provides a means of enabling them to meet the demands and cope with the stresses encountered in the family arena, and to cope with the guilt which arises from the women's self-blame for their lack of contentment.

Rosenbaum has argued that the career of the female drug user is one of 'narrowing options' in which even the options of wife and mother are closed off as women become more enmeshed in the world of addiction (Rosenbaum, 1981). Implicit in her argument is the notion that a career in the domestic sphere is a desirable and fulfilling career. From the evidence presented here, it can be seen that the women in Glasgow had very few options available to them from the outset. Rather than a career of narrowing options, the career of these working-class female drug users is one which highlights the capabilities of such women, albeit expressed in socially unacceptable ways, their implicit rejection of the narrow options laid down for them, including that of full-time wife and mother, and the inability of society either to recognize or to cater for such women's needs.

It would be good if drug users could be helped to fill their minds and imaginations with different things to do. Help them discover their true selves so that they didnae need anything at all. But I don't think anybody gets that help.   (Rose)

References

ADVISORY COUNCIL ON THE MISUSE OF DRUGS (1989). *AIDS and Drug Misuse*, *Part 2*. London: HMSO.

AGAR, M. (1973). *Ripping and Running*. New York: Seminar.

ALKSNE, H., LIEBERMAN L., and BRILL, L. (1967). 'A Conceptual Model of the Life Cycle of Addiction', *International Journal of the Addictions*, 2(2): 221–40.

ANGLIN, M. D. and HSER, Y. (1987). 'Addicted Women and Crime', *Criminology*, 25(2): 359–97.

ANTONIS, B. (1981). 'Motherhood and Mothering', in Cambridge Women's Studies Group, *Women in Society*. London: Virago.

AULD, J., DORN, N., and SOUTH, N. (1986). 'Irregular Work, Irregular Pleasures: Heroin in the 1980s', in R. Matthews and J. Young (eds.), *Confronting Crime*. London: Sage.

BADINTER, E. (1981). *The Myth of Motherhood*. London: Souvenir.

BALDINGER, R., GOLDSMITH, B. M., CAPEL, W. C., and STEWART, G. T. (1972). 'Pot Smokers, Junkies and Squares: A Comparative Study of Female Values', *International Journal of the Addictions*, 7(1): 153–66.

BAUMAN, P. (1980). 'A Controlled Study of Drug-Addicted Mothers' Parenting and Their Children's Development', diss., California School of Professional Psychology, Berkeley.

—— and DOUGHERTY, F. E. (1983). 'Drug-Addicted Mothers' Parenting and Their Children's Development', *International Journal of the Addictions*, 18(3): 291–302.

BEAN, P. T., and WILKINSON, C. K. (1988). 'Drug Taking, Crime and the Illicit Supply System', *British Journal of Addiction*, 83: 533–9.

BECKER, H. S. (1963). *Outsiders: Studies in the Sociology of Deviance*. New York: Free Press.

—— (1970*a*). 'Whose Side Are We On?', in W. J. Filstead (ed.), *Qualitative Methodology*. Chicago: Markham.

—— (1970*b*). 'Problems of Inference and Proof in Participant Observation', in W. J. Filstead (ed.), *Qualitative Methodology*, Chicago: Markham.

—— (1970*c*). *Sociological Work*. Chicago: Aldine.

BENNETT, T. (1990). 'Links Between Drug Misuse and Crime', *British Journal of Addiction*, 85: 833–5.

BERNARD, J. (1974). *The Future of Motherhood*. New York: Dial.

BILTON, T., BONNETT, K., JONES, P., SHEARD, K., STANWORTH, M., and WEBSTER, A. (1981). *Introductory Sociology*. Basingstoke: Macmillan Education.

BINION, V. J. (1979). 'A Descriptive Comparison of the Families of Origin of Women Heroin Users and Non-Users', in NIDA, 1979.

—— (1982). 'Sex Differences in Socialization and Family Dynamics of Female and Male Heroin Users', *Journal of Social Issues*, 38(2): 43–57.

BLACK, R., MAYER, J., and MACDONALL, J. (1978). 'Child Abuse and Neglect in Families with an Opiate Addicted Parent', in D. E. Smith, S. M. Anderson, M. Buxton, M. Gottlieb, W. Harvey, and T. Chung (eds.), *A Multicultural View of Drug Abuse: Proceedings of the National Drug Abuse Conference, 1977*. Cambridge, Mass: Schenkman.

BLENHEIM PROJECT (1988). *Changing Gear: A Book for Women Who Use Drugs Illegally*. London: Blenheim Project.

BLUMER, H. (1969). *Symbolic Interactionism*. Englewood Cliffs, NJ: Prentice-Hall.

BOULTON, M. G. (1983). *On Being A Mother: A Study of Women with Pre-School Children*. London: Tavistock.

BROWN, B. S., GAUVEY, S. K., MEYERS, M. B., and STARK, S. D. (1971). 'In Their Own Words: Addicts' Reasons for Initiating and Withdrawing from Heroin', *International Journal of the Addictions*, 6(4): 635–45.

BROWN, G., and HARRIS, T. (1978). *The Social Origins of Depression*. London: Tavistock.

BURGESS, R. G. (1982). 'Approaches to Field Research', in R. G. Burgess (ed.), *Field Research: A Sourcebook and Field Manual*. London: George Allen and Unwin.

BURNS, W. J. (1986). 'Psychopathology of Mother–Infant Interaction', in Chasnoff (1986*b*).

BURY, J. (1988). 'Prevention of HIV Infection: Education', in Women and AIDS (1988).

CANNON, S. (1989). 'Social Research in Stressful Settings: Difficulties for the Sociologist Studying the Treatment of Breast Cancer', *Sociology of Health and Illness*, 11(1): 62–77.

CARLEN, P. (1983). *Women's Imprisonment*. London: Routledge and Kegan Paul.

CARLSON, K. (1976). 'Heroin, Hassle, and Treatment: The Importance of Perceptual Differences', *Addictive Diseases: An International Journal*, 2(4): 569–84.

CARR, J. N. (1975). 'Drug Patterns Among Drug-Addicted Mothers: Incidence, Variance in Use, and Effects in Children', *Pediatric Annals* (July): 65–77.

CAVISTON, P. (1987). 'Pregnancy and Opiate Addiction', *British Medical Journal*, 295: 285.

CHAMBERS, C. D., HINESLEY, R. K., and MOLDESTAD, M. (1970). 'Narcotic Addiction in Females: A Race Comparison', *International Journal of the Addictions*, 5(2): 257–78.

CHAN, L. S., WINGERT, W. A., WACHSMAN, L., SCHUETZ, S., and ROGERS, C.

(1986). 'Differences Between Dropouts and Active Participants in a Pediatric Clinic for Substance Abuse Mothers', *American Journal of Drug Alcohol Abuse*, 12(1 and 2): 89–99.

CHASNOFF, I. J. (1986*a*). 'Perinatal Addiction: Consequences of Intrauterine Exposure to Opiate and Monopiate Drugs', in Chasnoff (1986*b*).

—— (ed.) (1986*b*). *Drug Use in Pregnancy: Mother and Child*. Lancaster: MTP.

CHEIN, I., GERARD, D. L., LEE, R. S., and ROSENFIELD, E. (1964). *Narcotics, Delinquency and Social Policy: The Road to H*. London: Tavistock.

CHETWYND, J., and HARTNETT, O. (eds.) (1978). *The Sex-Role System*. London: Routledge and Kegan Paul.

CHISUM, G. M. (1986). 'Recognition and Initial Management of the Pregnant Substance Abusing Woman', in Chasnoff (1986*b*).

CHOWDHURY, M. D., and CHOWDHURY, S. (1990). 'Buprenorphine Abuse: Report from India', *British Journal of Addiction*, 85: 1349–50.

CHRISTENSON, S. J., and SWANSON, A. Q. (1974). 'Women and Drug Use: An Annotated Bibliography', *Journal of Psychedelic Drugs*, 6(4): 371–414.

CHRISTMAS, J. J. (1978) 'Women, Alcohol and Drugs: Issues and Implications', in A. Schecter (ed.), *Drug Abuse: Modern Trends, Issues and Perspectives*. New York: Dekker.

CLOWARD, R., and OHLIN, L. (1960). *Delinquency and Opportunity*. New York: Free Press.

COHEN, J. B., HAUER, L. B., and WOLFSY, C. B. (1989). 'Women and IV Drugs: Parenteral and Heterosexual Transmission of Human Immunodeficiency Virus', *Journal of Drug Issues*, 19(1): 39–56.

COLTEN, M. E. (1979). 'A Descriptive and Comparative Analysis of Self-perceptions and Attitudes of Heroin-Addicted Women', in NIDA (1979).

—— (1982). 'Attitudes, Experiences and Self-Perceptions of Heroin-Addicted Mothers', *Journal of Social Issues*, 38(2): 77–92.

CONNORS, J. (1990). 'Women, Drug Control and the Law', *Bulletin on Narcotics*, 42(1): 41–7.

COOMBS, R. H., FRY, L. J., and LEWIS, P. G. (eds.) (1976). *Socialization in Drug Abuse*. Cambridge, Mass.: Schenkman.

COOPERSTOCK, R., and LENNARD, H. (1979). 'Some Social Meanings of Tranquiliser Use', *Sociology of Health and Illness*, 1(3): 331–47.

COUSINS, P., and BENTALL, R. P. (1989). 'Heroin Users' Careers and Perceptions of Drug Use: A Comparison of Smokers and Injectors in the Mersey Region', *British Journal of Addiction*, 84: 1467–72.

COVINGTON, J. (1985). 'Gender Differences in Criminality Among Heroin Users', *Journal of Research in Crime and Delinquency*, 22(4): 329–54.

—— (1988). 'Crime and Heroin: The Effects of Race and Gender', *Journal of Black Studies*, 18(4): 486–506.

COYLE, A. (1984). *Redundant Women*. London: Women's Press.

CUSHMAN, P. (1972). 'Methadone Maintenance Treatment of Narcotic

Addiction: Analysis of Police Records of Arrest Before and After Treatment', *New York State Journal of Medicine*, 72: 1752–69.

CUSKEY, W. R. (1982). 'Female Addiction: A Review of the Literature', *Journal of Addictions and Health*, 3(1): 3–33.

DAI, B. (1937). *Opium Addiction in Chicago*. Shanghai: Commercial Press.

DALLY, A. (1982). *Inventing Motherhood: The Consequences of an Ideal*. London: Burnett.

DATESMAN, S. K. (1981). 'Women, Crime and Drugs', in J. A. Inciardi (ed.), *The Drugs–Crime Connection*. Beverly Hills, Calif.: Sage.

—— and INCIARDI, J. A. (1979). 'Female Heroin Use, Criminality and Prostitution', *Contemporary Drug Problems* (winter): 455–73.

DE LEON, G. (1974). 'Phoenix House: Psychopathological Signs Among Male and Female Drug-Free Residents', *Addictive Diseases: An International Journal*, 1(2): 135–51.

DENSEN-GERBER, J., and ROHRS, C. C. (1973). 'Drug-Addicted Parents and Child Abuse', *Contemporary Drug Problems*, 2(4): 683–96.

—— WIENER, M., and HOCHSTEDLER, R. (1972). 'Sexual Behaviour, Abortion and Birth Control in Heroin Addicts: Legal and Psychiatric Considerations', *Contemporary Drug Problems*, 1: 783–93.

DEREN, S. (1986). 'Children of Substance Abusers: A Review of the Literature', *Journal of Substance Abuse Treatment*, 3: 77–94.

DITTON, J., and SPEIRITS, K. (1984). *The Rapid Increase of Heroin Addiction in Glasgow During 1981*. Glasgow: Dept. of Sociology, University of Glasgow.

—— and TAYLOR, A. (1987). *Scotland Drugs Resource Book 1980–1984*. Glasgow: Dept. of Sociology, University of Glasgow.

—— —— (1990). *Scotland's Drug-Misuse Agencies: 1987 Survey*. Central Research Unit Papers, Edinburgh: Scottish Office.

DOBASH, R., and DOBASH, R. (1980). *Violence Against Wives*. London: Open Books.

DONOGHOE, M., DORN, N., JAMES, C., JONES, S., RIBBENS, J., and SOUTH, N. (1987). 'How Families and Communities Respond to Heroin', in Dorn and South (1987).

DORN, N., RIBBENS, J., and SOUTH, N. (1987). *Coping With A Nightmare: Family Feelings About Long-Term Drug Use*. London: Institute for the Study of Drug Dependency.

—— and SOUTH, N. (1985). *Helping Drug Users: Social Work, Advice Giving, Referral and Training Services of Three London 'Street Agencies'*. Aldershot: Gower.

—— —— (eds.) (1987). *A Land Fit For Heroin? Drug Policies, Prevention and Practice*. Basingstoke: Macmillan Education.

—— —— (1990). 'Drug Markets and Law Enforcement', *British Journal of Criminology*, 30: 171–88.

DOSHAN, T., and BURSCH, C. (1982). 'Women and Substance Abuse: Critical Issues in Treatment Design', *Journal of Drug Education*, 12(3): 229–39.

DOUGLAS, J. D. (ed.) (1970). *Observations of Deviance*. New York: Random House.

—— (1972). 'Observing Deviance', in J. D. Douglas (ed.), *Research on Deviance*, New York: Random House.

DRUG INDICATORS PROJECT (1989). *Study of Help Seeking and Service Uitlisation by Problem Drug Takers*. London: Institute for the Study of Drug Dependence.

DRUMMOND, D. C. (1986). 'Substance Abuse Problems in Scotland', *Journal of Substance Abuse Treatment*, 3: 223–6.

DUELLI KLEIN, R. (1983). 'How to Do What We Want to Do: Thoughts About Feminist Methodology', in G. Bowles and R. Duelli Klein (eds.), *Theories of Women's Studies*. London: Routledge and Kegan Paul.

ELDRED, C. A., GRIER, V. V., and BERLINER, N. (1974). 'Comprehensive Treatment for Heroin Addicted Mothers', *Social Casework*, 55: 1450–77.

—— and WASHINGTON, M. N. (1976). 'Interpersonal Relationships in Heroin Use by Men and Women and Their Role in Treatment Outcome', *International Journal of the Addictions*, 11(1): 117–30.

ELLINWOOD, E. H., SMITH, W. G., and VAILLANT, G. E. (1966). 'Narcotic Addiction in Males and Females: A Comparison', *International Journal of the Addictions*, 1(2): 33–45.

ETTORE, B. (1985). 'Psychotropics, Passivity and the Pharmaceutical Industry', in A. Henman, R. Lewis, and T. Malyon with B. Ettore and L. O'Bryan, *Big Deal: The Politics of the Illicit Drug Business*. London: Pluto.

—— (1986). 'Women and Drunken Sociology: Developing a Feminist Analysis', *Women's Studies International Forum*, 9(5): 515–20.

—— (1989a). 'Women, Substance Abuse and Self-Help', in S. MacGregor (ed.), *Drugs and British Society*. London: Routledge.

—— (1989b). 'Women and Substance Use/Abuse: Towards a Feminist Perspective or How to Make Dust Fly', *Women's Studies International Forum*, 12(6): 593–602.

FAIRES, T. M. (1976/7). 'A Group Experience to Foster Mothering Skills in Drug Using Mothers', *Drug Forum*, 5(3): 229–35.

FARKAS, M. I. (1976). 'The Addicted Couple', *Drug Forum*, 5(1): 81–7.

FAUPEL, C. E. (1987). 'Drug Availability, Life Structure, and Situational Ethics of Heroin Addicts', *Urban Life*, 15(3 and 4): 395–419.

FELDMAN, H. W. (1968). 'Ideological Supports to Becoming and Remaining a Heroin Addict', *Journal of Health and Social Behaviour*, 9: 131–9.

FIDDLE, S. (1976). 'Sequences in Addiction', *Addictive Diseases: An International Journal*, 2(4): 553–68.

FIKS, K. B., JOHNSON, H. L., and ROSEN, T. S. (1985). 'Methadone-

Maintained Mothers: Three-Year Follow-Up of Parental Functioning', *International Journal of the Addictions*, 20(5): 651–60.

FILE, K. M. (1976). 'Sex Roles and Street Roles', *International Journal of the Addictions*, 11(2): 263–8.

—— MCCAHILL, T. W., and SAVITZ, L.D. (1974). 'Narcotics Involvement and Female Criminality', *Addictive Diseases: An International Journal*, 1(2): 177–88.

FINESTONE, H. (1957). 'Cats, Kicks and Color'; repr. in H. S. Becker (ed.) (1964), *The Other Side: Perspectives on Deviance*. New York: Free Press.

FINNEGAN, L. P. (1975). 'Narcotics Dependence in Pregnancy', *Journal of Psychedelic Drugs*, 7(3): 299–311.

—— (1981). 'Maternal and Neonatal Effects of Drug Dependence in Pregnancy', in J. H. Lowinson and P. Ruiz (eds.), *Substance Abuse: Clinical Problems and Perspectives*. Baltimore, Md.: Williams and Wilkins.

FITZSIMMONS, J., TUNIS, S., WEBSTER, D., ILES, J., WAPNER, R., and FINNEGAN, L. (1986). 'Pregnancy in a Drug Abusing Population', *American Journal of Drug Addiction Abuse*, 12(3): 247–55.

FRASER, A., and GEORGE, M. (1988). 'Changing Trends in Drug Use: An Initial Follow-Up of a Local Heroin Using Community', *British Journal of Addiction*, 83: 655–63.

FREEDMAN, T., WEINER, H., and FINNEGAN, L. P. (1978). 'The Family System of the Drug-Dependent Mother and Her Newborn', in A. Schecter (ed.), *Drug Abuse: Modern Trends, Issues and Perspectives*. New York: Dekker.

FRIEDMAN, A. S., GLICKMAN, N. W., and MORRISSEY, M. R. (1988). 'What Mothers Know About Their Adolescents' Alcohol/Drug Use and Problems and How Mothers React to Finding Out About It', *Journal of Drug Education*, 18(2): 155–67.

FRISCHER, M. (1992). 'Estimated Prevalence of Injecting Drug Use in Glasgow', *British Journal of Addiction*, 87: 235–43.

FULLER, M. (1978). 'Sex-Role Stereotyping and Social Science,' in Chetwynd and Hartnett (1978).

GANS, H. (1982). 'The Participant Observer as a Human Being: Observations in the Personal Aspects of Field Work', in R. G. Burgess (ed.), *Field Research: A Sourcebook and Field Manual*. London: George Allen and Unwin.

GERSTEIN, D. R., JUDD, L. L., and ROVNER, S. A. (1979). 'Career Dynamics of Female Heroin Addicts', *American Journal of Drug and Alcohol Abuse*, 6(1): 1–23.

GILMAN, M. (1988). 'Joining the Professionals', *Druglink* Mar./Apr.: 10–11.

GLASER, B. G., and STRAUSS, A. L. (1967). *The Discovery of Grounded Theory: Strategies for Qualitative Research*. Chicago: Aldine.

GLASGOW DISTRICT COUNCIL (1988). *Ward Profile*.

GOLD, R. L. (1969). 'Roles in Sociological Field Observations', in G. J.

McCall and J. L. Simmons (eds.), *Issues in Participant Observation: A Text*. Reading, Mass.: Addison Wesley.

GOLDSTEIN, P. J. (1979). *Prostitution and Drugs*. Lexington, Mass.: Lexington Books.

GOMBERG, E. S. L. (1986). 'Women: Alcohol and Other Drugs', *Drugs and Society*, 1(14): 75–109.

GOSSOP, M. (1986). 'Drug Dependence and Self-Esteem', *International Journal of the Addictions*, 11(5): 741–53.

GOULD, L. C., WALKER, A. L., CRANE, L. E., and LIDZ, C. W. (1974). *Connections: Notes from the Heroin World*. New Haven, Conn.: Yale University Press.

GRAHAM, H. (1982). 'Coping: Or How Mothers Are Seen and Not Heard', in S. Friedman and E. Sarah (eds.), *On The Problem of Men*. London: Women's Press.

GRAHAM, H. (1984). *Women, Health and the Family*. Brighton: Wheatsheaf.

—— and McKEE, L. (1980). *The First Months of Motherhood*. London: Health Education Council.

GRIFFIN-SHELLEY, E. (1986). 'Sex Roles in Addiction: Defense or Deficit?' *International Journal of the Addictions*, 21(12): 1307–12.

GRIFFITHS, R., and PEARSON, B. (1988). *Working With Drug Users*. Aldershot: Wildwood House.

HAMMERSLEY, R., FORSYTH, A., and LAVELLE, T. (1990). 'The Criminality of New Drug Users in Glasgow', *British Journal of Addiction*, 85: 1583–94.

—— —— MORRISON, V., and DAVIES, J. B. (1989). 'The Relationship Between Crime and Opioid Use', *British Journal of Addiction*, 84: 1029–43.

—— LAVELLE, T., and FORSYTH, A. (1990). 'Buprenorphine and Temazepam Abuse', *British Journal of Addiction*, 85: 301–3.

—— and MORRISON, V. L. (1987). 'Effects of Poly-Drug Use on the Criminal Activities of Heroin Users', *British Journal of Addiction*, 82: 899–906.

—— HAMMERSLEY, (1988). 'Crime Amongst Alcohol, Cannabis and Heroin Users', *Medicine and Law*, 7: 185–93.

HANSON, B., BESCHNER, G., WALTERS, J. M., and BOVELLE, E. (eds.) (1985). *Life With Heroin: Voices From The Inner City*. Lexington, Mass.: Lexington Books.

HARDING, G. (1988). 'Patterns of Heroin Use: What Do We Know?' *British Journal of Addiction*, 83: 1247–54.

HARDING, S. (1987). 'Introduction: Is There a Feminist Methodology?' in S. Harding (ed.), *Feminism and Methodology*. Milton Keynes: Open University Press.

HARTNOLL, R., and POWER, R. (1989). 'Why Most of Britain's Drug Users are Not Looking for Help', *Druglink* (Mar./Apr.): 8–9.

HAW, S. (1985). *Drug Problems in Greater Glasgow*. Glasgow: Standing Conference on Drug Abuse.

HENDERSON, S. (ed.) (1990). *Women, HIV, Drugs: Practical Issues*. London: Institute for the Study of Drug Dependency.

HEPBURN, M. (1990). 'Obstetrics, Drug Use and HIV', in Henderson (1990).

HOGG, C. (1989). *Drug Using Parents and Their Children: The Second Report of the National Local Authority Forum on Drug Misuse in Conjunction with the Standing Conference on Drug Abuse*. London: SCODA.

HOWARD, J., and BORGES, P. (1970). 'Needle Sharing in the Haight: Some Social and Psychological Functions', *Journal of Health and Social Behaviour*, 11: 220–30.

HSER, Y., ANGLIN, M. D., and BOOTH, M. W. (1987). 'Sex Differences in Addict Careers, 3: Addiction', *American Journal of Drug and Alcohol Abuse*, 13(3): 231–51.

HUGHES, E. G. (1960). 'Introduction: The Place of Field Work in Social Science', in B. H. Junker, *Field Work: An Introduction to the Social Sciences*. Chicago: University of Chicago Press.

HUGHES, P. H., CRAWFORD, G. A., BARKER, A. M., SCHUMANN, A. M. S., and JAFFE, J. H. (1971). 'The Social Structure of a Heroin Copping Community', *American Journal of Psychiatry*, 128(5): 551–8.

INCIARDI, J. A. (1980). 'Women, Heroin and Property Crime', in S. K. Datesman (ed.), *Women, Crime and Justice*. Oxford: Oxford University Press.

—— POTTIEGER, A. E., and FAUPEL, C. E. (1982). 'Black Women, Heroin and Crime: Some Empirical Notes', *Journal of Drug Issues*, 14: 91–106.

IRWIN, J. (1972). 'Participant Observation of Criminals', in J. D. Douglas (ed.), *Research On Deviance*. New York: Random House.

ISDD (Institute for the Study of Drug Dependence) Research and Development Unit (1987). 'Heroin Today: Commodity, Consumption, Control and Care', in Dorn and South (1987).

JAHODA, M. (1982). *Employment and Unemployment: A Social-Psychological Analysis*. Cambridge: Cambridge University Press.

JAMES, J. (1976). 'Prostitution and Addiction: An Interdisciplinary Approach', *Addictive Diseases: An International Journal*, 2(4): 601–18.

—— GOSHO, C. and WOHL, R. W. (1979). 'The Relationship Between Female Criminality and Drug Use', *International Journal of Addictions*, 14(2): 215–19.

JEFFRIES, S. (1983). 'Heroin Addiction: Beyond the Stereotype', *Spare Rib* (July): 6–8.

JOHNSON, B. D., GOLDSTEIN, P., PREBLE, E., SCHMEIDLER, J., LIPTON, D. S., SPUNT, B., and MILLER, T. (1985). *Taking Care of Business: The Economics of Crime by Heroin Abusers*. Lexington, Mass.: Lexington Books.

JOHNSON INSTITUTE (1988). *Alcohol/Drug Dependent Women: New Insights into Their Special Problems, Treatment, Recovery*. USA: Johnson Institute.

KAESTNER, E., FRANK, B., MAREL, R., and SCHMEIDLER, J. (1986). 'Substance

Use Among Females in New York State: Catching Up with the Males', *Advances in Alcohol and Substance Abuse*, 5(3): 29–49.

KAUFMAN, E. (1985). *Substance Abuse and Family Therapy*. New York: Grune and Stratton.

KEITH, L., DONALD, W., ROSHER, M., MITCHELL, M., and BIANCHI, J. (1986). 'Obstetric Aspects of Perinatal Addiction', in Chasnoff (1986b).

KITZINGER, S. (1978). *Women as Mothers*. Oxford: Martin Robertson.

KLEE, H., FAUGIER, J., HAYES, C., BOULTON, T., and MORRIS, J. (1990). 'AIDS-Related Risk Behaviour, Polydrug Use and Temazepam', *British Journal of Addiction*, 85: 1125–32.

KLENKA, H. (1986). 'Babies Born in a District General Hospital to Mothers Taking Heroin', *British Medical Journal* (Sept.): 745–6.

KOSTEN, T. R., NOVAK, P., and KLEBER, H. D. (1984). 'Perceived Marital and Family Environment of Opiate Addicts', *American Journal of Drug and Alcohol Abuse*, 10(4): 491–501.

KROLL, D. (1986). 'Heroin Addiction in Pregnancy', *Midwives' Chronicle and Nursing Notes* (July): 153–7.

LAWSON, M. S., and WILSON, G. S. (1980). 'Parenting Among Women Addicted to Narcotics', *Child Welfare*, 59: 67–79.

LEVIN, J. (1987). 'Will All Addicted Pregnant Women Have New Babies Taken into Care?', *Lancet*, 24 Jan., 230.

LEVY, S., and DOYLE, K. M. (1975). 'Attitudes Towards Women in a Drug Abuse Treatment Program', in E. Senay, V. Shorty, and H. Alksne (eds.) *Developments in the Field of Drug Abuse*, 503–4. Cambridge, Mass: Schenkman.

LIEF, N. R. (1985). 'The Drug User as Parent', *International Journal of the Addictions*, 20(1): 63–97.

LINDESMITH, A. R. (1968). *Addiction and Opiates*. Chicago: Aldine.

LONDON HOSPITAL WOMEN'S GROUP (1976/7). 'Drugs and Women', *Undercurrents*, 19: 34–5.

McGRATH, J. E. (1982). Editorial, *Journal of Social Issues*, 38(2).

MacGREGOR, S., and ETTORE, B. (1987). 'From Treatment to Rehabilitation: Aspects of the Evolution of British Policy on the Care of Drug-Takers', in Dorn and South (1987).

McKEGANEY, N. (1990). 'Being Positive: Drug Injectors' Experiences of HIV Infection', *British Journal of Addiction*, 85: 113–24.

McKEGANEY, N. P., and BODDY, F. A. (1987). *Drug Abuse in Glasgow: An Interim Report of an Exploratory Study*. University of Glasgow: Social, Paediatric and Obstetric Research Unit.

MALINOWSKI, B. (1922). *Argonauts of the Western Pacific*. London: Routledge and Kegan Paul.

MANDEL, L., SCHULMAN, J., and MONTEIRO, R. (1979). 'A Feminist Approach for the Treatment of Drug-Abusing Women in a Coed Therapeutic Community', *International Journal of the the Addictions*, 14(5): 589–97.

MANN, F. C. (1970). 'Human Relations Skills in Social Research', in W. J. Filstead, *Qualitative Methodology*. Chicago: Markham.

MARSH, J. C. (1982). 'Public Issues and Private Problems: Women and Drug Use', *Journal of Social Issues*, 38(2): 153–65.

—— COLTEN, M. E., and TUCKER, M. B. (1982). 'Women's Use of Drugs and Alcohol: New Perspectives', *Journal of Social Issues*, 38(2): 1–8.

MARSH, K. L., and SIMPSON, D. D. (1986). 'Sex Differences in Opioid Addiction Careers', *American Journal of Drug and Alcohol Abuse*, 12(4): 309–29.

MARSHALL, N., and HENDTLASS, J. (1986). 'Drugs and Prostitution', *Journal of Drug Issues*, 16(2) 237–48.

MARTIN, C. A., and MARTIN, W. R. (1980). 'Opiate Dependence In Women', in O. J. Kalant (ed.), *Alcohol and Drug Problems In Women: Research Advances in Alcohol and Drug Problems*, v. New York: Plenum.

MARTIN, R., and WALLACE, J. (1984). *Working Women in Recession*. Oxford: Oxford University Press.

MATTHEWS, L. (1990). Book Review, *International Journal of Drug Policy*, 2(3): 30–1.

MAYER, J., and BLACK, R. (1977). 'Child Abuse and Neglect in Families with an Alcohol and Opiate Addicted Parent', *Child Abuse and Neglect*, 1: 85–98.

MAYNARD, M. (1990). 'The Re-Shaping of Sociology? Trends in the Study of Gender', *Sociology*, 24(2): 269–90.

MEAD, G. H. (1939). *Mind, Self and Society*. Chicago: University of Chicago Press.

MERRICK, J. (1985). 'Addicted Mothers and Their Children: Research Results from Denmark', *International Journal of Rehabilitation Research*, 8(1): 79–84.

MILLETT, K. (1975). *The Prostitution Papers*. St Albans: Paladin.

MILLS, C. W. (1940). 'Situated Actions and Vocabularies of Motive', *American Sociological Review*, 5: 904–13.

MONDANARO, J. (1989). *Chemically Dependent Women: Assessment and Treatment*. Lexington, Mass.: Lexington Books.

MORABIA, A., FABRE, J., CHEE, E., ZEGAR, S., ORSAT, E., and ROBERT, A. (1989). 'Diet and Opiate Addiction: A Quantitative Assessment of the Diet of Non-Institutionalised Opiate Addicts', *British Journal of Addiction*, 84: 173–80.

MORGAN-THOMAS, R. (1990). 'AIDS Risks, Alcohol, Drugs and the Sex Industry: A Scottish Study' in Plant (1990).

MORRISON, V. (1988). 'Observation and Snowballing: Useful Tools for Research Into Illicit Drug Use', *Social Pharmacology*, 2: 245–71.

—— (1989). 'Psychoactive Substance Use and Related Behaviour of 135 Regular and Illicit Drug Users in Scotland', *Drug and Alcohol Dependence*, 23: 95–101.

—— and PLANT, M. (1990). 'Drug Problems and Patterns of Service Use amongst Illicit Drug Users in Edinburgh', *British Journal of Addiction*, 85: 547–54.

MURPHY, P. N., BENTALL, R. P., and OWENS, R. G. (1989). 'The Experience of Opioid Abstinence: The Relevance of Motivation and History', *British Journal of Addiction*, 84: 673–9.

NEWS RELEASE (1979). 'Women and Drugs', *News Release* (summer): 8–11.

NIDA (NATIONAL INSTITUTE ON DRUG ABUSE) SERVICES (1979). *Addicted Women: Family Dynamics, Self-Perceptions and Support Systems*. DHEW Publications No. ADM 80–762. Washington, DC: US Govt Printing Office.

OAKLEY, A. (1974). *Housewife*. London: Allen Lane.

—— (1979). *Becoming A Mother*. Oxford: Martin Robertson.

—— (1980). *Women Confined: Towards a Sociology of Childbirth*. Oxford: Martin Robertson.

O'BRYAN, L. (1989). 'Young People and Drugs', in S. MacGregor (ed.), *Drugs and British Society*. London: Routledge.

O'CONNOR, J. J., MOLONEY, E., TRAVERS, R., and CAMPBELL, M. B. (1988). 'Buprenorphine Abuse among Opiate Addicts', *British Journal of Addiction*, 83: 1085–7.

O'DONOHUE, M., and RICHARDSON, S. (eds.) (1984). *Pure Murder . . . A Book About Drug Use*. Dublin: Women's Community Press.

ONG, T.-H. (1989). 'Peers as Perceived by Drug Abusers in their Drug-Seeking Behaviour', *British Journal of Addiction*, 84: 631–7.

OPPENHEIMER, E., SHEEHAN, M., and TAYLOR, C. (1988). 'Letting the Client Speak: Drug Misusers and the Process of Help Seeking', *British Journal of Addiction*, 83: 635–47.

d'ORBAN, P. T. (1970). 'Heroin Dependence and Delinquency in Women: A Study of Heroin Addicts in Holloway Prison', *British Journal of Addiction*, 65: 67–78.

OTTENBERG, M. (1975). 'Like The Song Says', in E. Senay, V. Shorty, and H. Alksne, (eds.), *Developments in the Field of Drug Abuse*. Cambridge, Mass.: Schenkman.

PARKER, H., BAKX, K., and NEWCOMBE, R. (1988). *Living With Heroin*. Milton Keynes: Open University Press.

PEAK, J. L., and GLANKOFF, P. (1975). 'The Female Patient as Booty', in E. Senay, V. Shorty, and H. Alksne, *Developments in the Field of Drug Abuse*. Cambridge, Mass.: Schenkman.

PEARSON, G. (1987a) *The New Heroin Users*. Oxford: Basil Blackwell.

—— (1987b). 'Social Deprivation, Unemployment and Patterns of Heroin Use', in Dorn and South (1987).

—— (1988). 'When Time Falls Apart', *Druglink*, (Mar./Apr.): 10.

—— GILMAN, M., and McIVER, S. (1986). *Young People and Heroin: An*

Examination of Heroin Use in the North of England. London: Health Education Council.

PECK, D. F., and PLANT, M. A. (1986). 'Unemployment and Illegal Drug Use', *British Medical Journal*, 293 (11 Oct): 929–31.

PERRY, L. (1979). *Women and Drug Use: An Unfeminine Dependency.* London: Institute for the Study of Drug Dependency.

—— (1987). 'Fit to Be Parents?' *Druglink* (Jan./Feb.): 6.

PLANT, M. (1990). 'Sex Work, Alcohol, Drugs and AIDS', in M. Plant (ed.), *AIDS, Drugs and Prostitution.* London: Tavistock/Routledge.

PLANT, M. A., and REEVES, C. E. (1976). 'Participant Observation as a Method of Collecting Information about Drug-Taking: Conclusions from Two English Studies', *British Journal of Addiction*, 71: 155–9.

POLIT, D. F., NUTTALL, R. L., and HUNTER, J. B. (1976). 'Women and Drugs: A Look at Some of the Issues', *Urban Social Change Review*, 9(2): 9–16.

POLSKY, N. (1969). *Hustlers, Beats and Others.* Harmondsworth: Penguin.

POWER, R. (1989). 'Participant Observation and its Place in the Study of Illicit Drug Abuse', *British Journal of Addiction*, 84: 43–52.

PRATHER, J. E. (1981). 'Women's Use of Licit and Illicit Drugs', in J. H. Lowinson and P. Ruiz (eds.), *Substance Abuse: Clinical Problems and Perspectives.* Baltimore, Md.: Williams and Wilkins.

—— and FIDELL, L. S. (1978). 'Drug Use and Abuse among Women: An Overview', *International Journal of the Addictions*, 13(6): 863–85.

PREBLE, E., and CASEY, J. J. (1969). 'Taking Care of Business: The Heroin User's Life on the Street', *International Journal of the Addictions*, 4(1): 1–24.

RAPOPORT, R. (1978). 'Sex-Role Stereotyping in Studies of Marriage and the Family', in Chetwynd and Hartnett (1978).

RAY, B. A., and BRAUDE, M. C. (1986). *Women and Drugs: A New Era for Research.* Rockville, Md.: NIDA.

RAY, M. B. (1964). 'The Cycle of Abstinence and Relapse Among Heroin Addicts', repr. in R. H. Coombs, L. J. Fry, and P. G. Lewis (eds.), *Socialization in Drug Abuse.* Cambridge, Mass.: Schenkman.

REED, B. G. (1985). 'Drug Misuse and Dependency in Women: The Meaning and Implications of Being Considered a Special Population or Minority Group', *International Journal of the Addictions*, 20(1): 13–62.

RICHARDSON, D. (1987). *Women and the AIDS Crisis.* London: Pandora.

ROBERTS, H. (1981). 'Women and their Doctors: Power and Powerlessness in the Research Process', in H. Roberts (ed.), *Doing Feminist Research.* London: Routledge and Kegan Paul.

ROBERTSON, R. (1987). *Heroin, AIDS And Society.* London: Hodder and Stoughton.

ROSENBAUM, M. (1979). 'Difficulties in Taking Care of Business: Women Addicts as Mothers', *American Journal of Drug and Alcohol Abuse*, 6(4): 431–46.

—— (1981). *Women on Heroin*. Brunswick, NJ: Rutgers University Press.

—— and MURPHY, S. (1984). 'Always A Junkie? The Arduous Task of Getting Off Methadone Maintenance', *Journal of Drug Issues*, 14(4): 527–52.

ROSS, H. E., GLASER, F. B., and STIASNY, S. (1988). 'Sex Differences in the Prevalence of Psychiatric Disorders in Patients with Alcohol and Drug Problems', *British Journal of Addiction*, 83: 1179–92.

ROSSI, A. (1973). 'Materialism, Sexuality and the New Feminism', in J. Zubin and J. Money (eds.), *Contemporary Sexual Behaviour: Critical Issues in the 1970s*. Baltimore Md.: Johns Hopkins University Press.

ROTH, J. (1963). *Timetables*. New York: Bobbs-Merrill.

RUBEN, S. (1990). 'Drug Dependency Units', in Henderson (1990).

RUBINGTON, E. (1967). 'Drug Addiction as a Deviant Career', *International Journal of the Addictions*, 2(1): 3–20.

RYAN, V. S., and MOISE, R. (1979). *A Comparison of Men and Women Entering Drug Abuse Treatment Programs*. Ann Arbor, Mich.: University of Michigan Press.

SAKOL, M. S., STARK, C., and SYKES, R. (1989). 'Buprenorphine and Temazepam Abuse by Drug Takers in Glasgow: An Increase', *British Journal of Addiction*, 84(4): 439–41.

SCHASRE, R. (1966). 'Cessation Patterns Among Neophyte Heroin Users', *International Journal of the Addictions*, 1(2): 23–32.

SCHATZMAN, L., and STRAUSS, A. (1973). *Field Research: Strategies for a Natural Sociology*. Englewood Cliffs, NJ: Prentice-Hall.

SCHULTZ, A. M. (1974). 'Radical Feminism', in E. Senay, V. Shorty, and H. Alskne (eds.) *Developments in the Field of Drug Abuse*. Cambridge, Mass.: Schenkman.

SCOTTISH DRUGS FORUM (1989). 'AIDS—HIV Positive Women: The Important Issues', *Scottish Drugs Forum Bulletin*, 25: 7.

SEN, A. (1984). *Resources, Values and Development*. Oxford: Basil Blackwell.

SHAFFIR, W. B., STEBBINS, R. A., and TUROWETZ, A. (1980). *Fieldwork Experience: Qualitative Approaches to Social Research*. New York: St Martin's Press.

SHAPIRO, H. (1989). *Drugs, Pregnancy and Childcare: A Guide for the Professionals*. London: Institute for the Study of Drug Dependency.

SILVER, F. C., PANEPINTO, W. C., ARNON, D., and SWAINE, W. T. (1975). 'A Family Approach in Treating the Pregnant Addict', in E. Senay, V. Shorty, and H. Alksne, (eds.) *Developments in the Field of Drug Abuse*. Cambridge, Mass.: Schenkman.

SILVERMAN, I. J. (1982). 'Women, Crime and Drugs', *Journal of Drug Issues*, 12(2): 167–83.

SINGER, A. (1974). 'Mothering Practices and Heroin Addiction', *American Journal of Nursing*, 74(1): 77–82.

SLOAN, A., and MURPHY, D. (1989). 'Drug Treatment During Pregnancy', *Mersey Drugs Journal*, 2(3): 15–16.

SMITHBERG, N., and WESTERMEYER, J. (1985). 'White Dragon Pearl Syndrome: A Female Pattern of Drug Dependence', *American Journal of Drug and Alcohol Abuse*, 11(3 and 4): 199–207.

SONNEX, C. (1987). 'Contraception and the Injecting Opiate User', *British Journal of Family Planning*, 13: 133–5.

SPRADLEY, J. P. (1980). *Participant Observation*. New York: Holt, Rinehart and Winston.

STANTON, M. D. (1979). 'Drugs and the Family', *Marriage and Family Review*, 2(1): 1–10.

STEWART, T. (1987). *The Heroin Users*. London: Pandora.

STIMSON, G. U., and OPPENHEIMER, E. (1982). *Heroin Addiction: Treatment and Control in Britain*. London: Tavistock.

STONE, M. L., SALERMO, L. J., GREEN, M., and ZELSON, C. (1971). 'Narcotic Addiction in Pregnancy', *American Journal of Obstetrics and Gynaecology*, 109(5): 716–23.

SUFFET, F., and BROTMAN, R. (1976). 'Female Drug Use: Some Observations', *International Journal of the Addictions*, 11(1): 19–33.

SUTTER, A. G. (1966). 'The World of the Righteous Dope Fiend', *Issues in Criminology*, 2(2): 177–222.

SWADI, H., WELLS, B., and POWER, R. (1990). 'Misuse of Dihydrocodeine Tartrate (DF118) Among Opiate Addicts', *British Medical Journal*, 300 (19 May): 131.

TUCKER, M. B. (1979). *A Descriptive and Comparative Analysis of the Social Support Structure of Heroin Addicted Women*. DHEW Publications No. ADM 80–762. Washington, DC: US Govt Printing Office.

—— (1982). 'Social Support and Coping: Applications for the Study of Female Drug Abuse', *Journal of Social Issues*, 38(2):117–39.

TYLER, J., and THOMPSON, M. (1980). 'Patterns of Drug Abuse Among Women', *International Journal of the Addictions*, 15(3): 309–21.

UNELL, I. (1987). 'Drugs and Deprivation', *Druglink* (Nov./Dec.): 14–15.

VAN DEN BERG, T., and BLOM, M. (1985). 'A Typology of Life and Work Styles of "Heroin-Prostitutes": From a Male Career Model into a Feminised Career Model', A. De Graaf Stichting, Westermarkt 4, 1016 DK Amsterdam.

VENEMA, P. U., and VISSER, J. (1990). 'Safer Prostitution: A New Approach in Holland', in Plant (1990).

WALBY, C. (1987). 'Addicted: Unborn Babies at Risk', *Community Care*, 15 Jan. 18–20.

WALDORF, D. (1970). 'Life Without Heroin: Some Social Adjustments During Long-Term Periods of Voluntary Abstention', *Social Problems*, 18: 228–43. repr. in Coombs *et al*. (1976: 365–85).

—— (1973). *Careers In Dope*. Englewood Cliffs, NJ: Prentice-Hall.

WAX, R. H. (1979). 'Gender and Age in Fieldwork Education: No Good Thing Is Done by Any Man Alone', *Social Problems*, 26(5): 509–22.

WEBER, M. (1947). *The Theory of Social and Economic Organization*, trans. A. Henderson and T. Parsons. Chicago: Free Press.

WEBSTER, P. (1984). 'The Forbidden: Eroticism and Taboo', in C. Vance (ed.). *Pleasure and Danger: Exploring Female Sexuality*. London: Routledge and Kegan Paul.

WEINBERG, M. S., and WILLIAMS, C. J. (1972). 'Fieldwork Among Deviants: Social Relations with Subjects and Others', in J. D. Douglas (ed.), *Research on Deviance*. New York: Random House.

WEISBERG, D. K. (1985). *Children of the Night: A Study of Adolescent Prostitution*. Lexington, Mass.: Lexington Books.

WELLISCH, D. K., GAY, G. R., and McENTEE, R. (1970). 'The Easy Rider Syndrome: A Pattern of Hetero- and Homosexual Relationships in a Heroin Addict Population', *Family Process*, 9(4): 425–30.

WHYTE, W. F. (1945). *Street Corner Society*. Chicago: University of Chicago Press.

WILLIAMS, T. (1989). *The Cocaine Kids*. Reading, Mass.: Addison Wesley.

WILSON, G. (1987). 'Money: Patterns of Responsibility and Irresponsibility in Marriage', in J. Brannen and G. Wilson (eds.), *Give and Take in Families: Studies in Resource Distribution*. London: Allen and Unwin.

WILSON, G. S., McCREARY, R., KEAN, J., and BAXTER, S. C. (1979). 'The Development of Pre-School Children and Heroin-Addicted Mothers: A Controlled Study', *Pediatrics*, 63(1): 135–41.

WOLFSON, D., and MURRAY, J. (eds.) (1986). *Women and Dependency*. London: DAWN.

WOMEN AND AIDS (1988). *Needs, Issues, Awareness*. Transcripts, workshop notes, and feedback from a one-day conference (May), Edinburgh.

WOMEN, HIV/AIDS NETWORK (1989). *Proceedings of Second National Conference*. (Oct.), Edinburgh.

WOMEN 2000 (1987). 'Women and Drug Abuse', *Women 2000*, 2: 1–18.

ZELSON, C. (1973). 'Infant of the Addicted Mother', *New England Journal of Medicine*, 288: 1393–5.

ZINBERG N. E. (1984). *Drug, Set and Setting*. New Haven, Conn.: Yale University Press.

Glossary

This glossary is intended to help the reader understand some of the words and phrases used by the women in the main body of the text. It includes words and phrases which are peculiarly Glaswegian or Scottish and therefore used by non-drug users as well as drug users. It also includes the argot associated with drug use. The definitions apply to the contexts in which the reader finds them, and may therefore not correspond either to the argot found in other drug texts or to definitions in texts devoted to Glaswegian or Scottish terminology.

aboot (prep./adv.)	about
acid (n.)	LSD
aff (prep./adv.)	off
aff her/his nut	she/he is stupid, crazy
ain (a.)	own
arenae (v.)	are not
aye	yes
batter (v.)	get rid of
beelin' (a.)	very angry
boggin' (a.)	extremely dirty, unkempt
boke, bokin' (v.)	vomit, vomiting
brand-new (a.)	excellent, wonderful
broo (n.)	Department of Employment, Department of Social Security (from Glaswegian pronunciation of 'bureau'—a former name for the Department of Employment)
bump (v.)	steal, fiddle, defraud
burlin' (v.)	whirling round
cannae (v.)	cannot
clathes (n.)	clothes
close (n.)	common entrance to block of flats or tenement building
cold turkey (v.)	withdraw from drugs suddenly and without using other drugs for relief of withdrawal symptoms

crackin' (a.)	wonderful, excellent, terrific
crackpot (n.)	stupid person
dae, dae'in (v.)	do, doing
darts team (back in the)	to return to intravenous drug use
dead (a.)	very
dead moaney (a.)	constantly complaining
deal (n.)	an amount of drugs
deid (a.)	dead
DFs/DF118s/Difs (n.)	dihydrocodeine
dicanol (n.)	dipipanone
didnae (v.)	did not
doon (prep./adv.)	down
dope (n.)	cannabis
downers (n.)	tranquillizers
eggs (n.)	temazepam (so called because temazepam is manufactured in the form of an egg-shaped capsule)
feart (a.)	afraid, frightened
frae (prep.)	from
full of it (a.)	heavily under the influence of drugs
gie (v.)	give
Glesga (n.)	Glasgow
graft, grafting (n./v.)	work, working
greet, greetin' (v.)	cry, crying
hame (n.)	home
hash (n.)	cannabis
hauf (n./a.)	half
heid (n.)	head
heid's nippin'	sore head, headache (*my heid's nippin'*: I have a sore head)
hen (n.)	term of affection for a girl or woman
hep (n.)	hepatitis
hit, hitting up (n./v.)	inject, injecting
hoose (n.)	house, flat, apartment
hurl, hurlin' (v.)	throw, throwing
jag, jaggin' (n./v.)	injection, inject, injecting
jellies (n.)	temazepam (so called because of the soft jelly-like substance inside the capsule)
junk (n.)	heroin

junkie (n.)	a person dependent on drugs, a drug addict
kit (n.)	heroin
lassie (n.)	girl
lay on (n.)	a loan of drugs from a dealer. Sometimes items such as jewellery are requested by the dealer as a 'pledge' to be redeemed when the money owed is paid
lug (n.)	ear
magic (a.)	wonderful, excellent, terrific
mair (a./adv.)	more
maist, maistly (a./adv.)	most, mostly
messages (n.)	shopping
nae (a.)	no (as in no money, nowhere, no one, etc.). At the end of a word (*cannae*, *couldnae*) it means 'not'
nippy (a.)	burning to the taste, sharp-tasting
no' (adv.)	not
no danger	not a chance
noo (adv.)	now
nut (n.)	head
oot (prep.)	out
pap, papping (v.)	give, throw; giving, throwing
poke (n.)	paper bag
polis (n.)	police
punt, punting (v.)	sell, selling
pure scream (n.)	A laugh, funny incident or happening
rattle, rattlin' (v.)	Suffer, suffering withdrawal symtoms
rehab (n.)	residential drug rehabilitation centre
rubbered (v.)	treated badly
score, scoring (v.)	purchase, purchasing drugs
score deal (n.)	£20 of heroin
scunner (v.)	sicken, disgust
script (n.)	prescription from doctor
selt (v.)	sold
skint (a.)	having no money
slabbering (v.)	drooling, dribbling
smack (n.)	heroin
spew, spewing (v.)	vomit, vomiting

square (me) up (v.) take enough drugs to stop, get rid of withdrawal symptoms, but not enough to feel euphoric

stone(d) (n./a.) drug-induced euphoria, heavily drugged.

straight (n.) non-drug user

straight (a.) drug-free

straighten (me) up (v.) take enough drugs to stop, get rid of, withdrawals, but not enough to feel euphoric

strung oot (a.) suffer withdrawal symtoms

tan, tanned (v.) steal, burgle; stole, burgled

tap, tappin' (v.) borrow, borrowing (usually money)

telt (v.) told

temgesic, tems (n.) buprenorphine

tenner bag (n.) £10 worth of heroin

toon (n.) town

turn (n.) theft (*he did/got a turn*: he stole, burgled)

turn on (n./v.) free sample of drugs; to introduce someone to drug-taking

wasnae (v.) was not

wean (n.) child (pronounced 'wane')

wee (a.) little, small

whit (a./pron.) what

work(ing) up the toon A euphemism for prostitution (refers to working location of most street prostitutes in Glasgow)

works (n.) needles, syringes, apparatus for intravenous drug use

Index